Journey to God

Journey to God

◆

...the last stretch

Marian Barasch

Writers Club Press
New York Lincoln Shanghai

Journey to God
...the last stretch

Writers Club Press
an imprint of iUniverse, Inc.

For information address:
iUniverse, Inc.
2021 Pine Lake Road, Suite 100
Lincoln, NE 68512
www.iuniverse.com

ISBN: 0-595-25777-1

Printed in the United States of America

*To my beloved wife Shari, who has with faith
and patience supported me in all my endeavors.*

Contents

Prologue

"He who knows eternity is called enlightened."

—Lao-Tzu

This book is neither a scientific manual nor a theological thesis. It is written for the person who can understand that even though we live in the present, each living moment carries the effects of the previous moment's action and that any future moment will be affected by the present decision. This continuous flow of moments is the definition of life. Any flow requires continuity and support. When excessive materialism is being worshipped, and theism is becoming a fanatic indoctrination with distorted religious beliefs, it cannot be stressed enough that the end of human existence is in sight.

This book is for the reader who is ready to understand, that he inhabits this planet as a member of a community of people, whose living rights must be respected, without disturbing the other species. Hate, greed, and deceit always lead to misery and war. At this point in evolution, the human species, through the irrational misuse of its intelligence, can destroy in a very short period of time what has taken thousands of years to build. An all-out nuclear confrontation is no longer a viable alternative. It would be the end of our fragile planet. The enrichment of each human soul is the only rational means by which to prolong mankind's future. It must be clear that because man has assumed the role of the dominant species in nature, he must rise from the lowest level of battle for survival to the highest level of human cooperation, while protecting the entire ecosystem. Tyranny has failed in all its forms. The recent democratization of the world's financial markets

1

constitutes the economic precursor of the major political tide of international freedom. Seemingly impossible, *globalism* must replace nationalism in the future.

In this modern age, computers and robots are programmed to do many laborious chores. It is a wonderful opportunity by which to learn to live by proven principles based on a sturdy alloy of exciting scientific discoveries and historically tested beliefs, thus elevating humanity to new levels of development. As democracy spreads across the planet, the understanding of the meaning of freedom plays a crucial role in this process. Freedom implies a multitude of choices. Correct action can be chosen based only on the capacity to discriminate between enrichment and destruction. Now is the time to choose. We can decimate each other through wars and starvation, and in so doing destroy our planet. We can continue to pollute the environment, and as the polar caps melt due to the greenhouse effect, hand our planet back to the dinosaurs, or we can embark upon a serious and honest review of our position in the Universe. Freedom can be a blessing for the enlightened, or in the hands of the unknowledgeable, a means by which to destroy the world. We have unintentionally entered the race for self-destruction. The time has come to regain our sense of direction, and pursue the ever-distancing goal of happiness for all mankind. The meaning of our existence implies a sustained collective effort to survive and share the remaining resources of the Earth. Wisdom and tolerance must triumph over ignorance and egocentrism. The use of all available means by which to enrich the world with positively charged souls is our only legacy to safeguard the future of life on Earth.

In this new millennium of flourishing freedom in arts and sciences, we are responsible for making choices that are much more difficult than ever before. We can never forget that we are temporary tenants, not owners of the planet. This book is a reminder for the affluent and the needy, for the materialist and the idealist, to select the correct pathway in the present maze of available options. I hope that after internalizing the immediate need for individual restraint from natural and social destruction, the human race will take the lead in the effort to prolong the last stretch of what was meant to be an endless journey towards perfection.

1

The Reason

"The most incomprehensible thing about the world is that it is comprehensible."

—*Albert Einstein*

I n one-way or another, human beings are looking for absolute happiness and an endless earthly life. Physics, using the language of mathematics, is trying to find a unified theory. Philosophy, using the power of logic, is trying to explain the meaning of life. Religion, using various dogmas, is promising conditional access to eternity. Nirvana is promised by Buddhist philosophy for the pure spirit, while the union with Universal Consciousness is promised in Hinduism. The monotheistic religions of Judaism, Christianity, and Islam present immortality in various ways. According to Jewish tradition, the most important task of every human being is to follow God in this world (olam hazeh), while the next world is a mystery in his hands. After their passing, Christian believers go to an eternal resting place where there is "a pure river of water of life, clear as crystal, proceeding out of the throne of God and of the Lamb. In the midst of the street of it, and on either side of the river, was there a tree of life, which bare twelve manner of fruits, and yielded her fruit every month; and the leaves of the tree were for the healing of the nations" *(Revelation 22:1,2).* In the Qur'an, the "Parable of the Garden" depicts metaphorically the place where the faithful go. According to *Surah 47:15*, it is a place of continuous joy for those who drink from rivers of milk, wine, and honey with a never changing taste.

The Universe is continuously changing. However, the human view of the divine is quasi-static. Our attempts to find "absolute happiness" have not proven to be successful, even though we have the most sophisticated tools available. Absolute happiness will always remain an elusive horizon toward which man will strive during his evolution. We will continue to achieve higher levels of knowledge as more subjects open to future research. The more we break down and analyze our overwhelming volume of data, the closer we get to the conclusion that what sciences refer to as "perfection" is the same as what religions call "God." To describe these concepts in spoken language is impossible. To feel their presence and be a part of them is "absolute happiness." The physicist who tries to understand the cosmos and succeeds in producing a new theory, and the believer who places his trust in a theological doctrine of moral life are living the dream, which life is meant to be. Many people will never know it, while true seekers can come close to it many times. It is all a matter of turning off the external stimuli and opening the mind to the built-in antenna.

To survive as the dominating species in the ever-evolving natural environment, man must continue to develop. We are close to the finish line in the long race for adaptation and survival on the planet. We also have the necessary tools by which to prolong our journey in time or to bring it to a sudden halt. With the development of modern technology, the communication revolution is bringing the world closer and we can spread ideas across long distances in a short time. However, our increasing knowledge has also led to the widespread availability of "intelligent" weapons of mass destruction, which sets us further apart. Rogue governments throughout the world are always ready to use them, thus hoping to fulfill their tyrannical dreams. By misleading their citizens and through the misinterpretation of religious beliefs, their leaders continuously threaten our survival. Fanatical doctrines, totalitarian systems of government, terror-promoting groups, irresponsible environmental policies, racism, and a lack of tolerance are the surest ways of losing everything that humanity has achieved so far. The destruction of available natural resources rather than the development of respect for our natural environment have recently intensified. The use of language for concealing the truth rather than striving to attain it has become a common practice. The lack of faith in our fellow man and our stubborn refusal to forgive are becoming more prevalent. The quest for "instant happiness" caused by man's incorrect use of knowledge has led us to the destructive use of technology. Arsenals of weapons of mass destruction are being built around the globe, as irresponsible parties seek world supremacy. These are dangerous currents pulling us rapidly toward the obliteration of our planet. The understanding and the preservation of the Earth in the eternal Universe are more important now than ever. Man has to remember that in the court of life, nature will always remain a "hanging judge." Empowering man's faculty of reason is the only remaining way for the world community to cooperate in a sustained ethical effort to guide humanity toward a prolonged existence within social systems based on freedom. Reason brought the human species to its present dominating position, while the lack of it will bring its destruction. As a part of the Universe, each of us must either succeed to be on, or be helped to get on the only road to achieve our personal dreams, avoid pain, and not hurt the perfect Universal order that maintains us.

According to George Santayana, a pioneer in critical realism, "repetition is the only form of permanence that nature can achieve." It is true that all chemical elements have been recycled millions of times. No one knows whose bones are concentrated in the classroom chalk. An idealistic parallel would be the recycling of our souls as a principle. A new theory of eternal existence based on conservation and recycling of life energy will be presented. It is based on sound principles, which have stood the test of time, and can help mankind prolong the last stretch of what was meant to be an eternal journey, thus postponing the inevitable destruction of the planet.

In the most general form, energy can be defined as the ability to cause an action. This action does not necessarily have to be, as the traditional definition states, work. Action transcends the definition used in physics and engineering, where work is only the physical effort needed to achieve a task. It can be assumed that no one wants to die, as proven by our constant advances in biotechnology, which are meant to prolong our physical lives. It is also known that in nature everything is cyclical. As the German physicist Johannes Kepler put it, "nature uses as little as possible of anything." Thus, within the oneness of the Universe, it seems reasonable to look beyond physical death and envision the recycling principle applied to the spirit as an integral part of existence. Similar to Gödel's Incompleteness Theorem applied to arithmetic, the complete capturing of the truth under previously accepted assumptions and logical rules, when applied to the Universal existence lead to one true statement that cannot be proven. No reliable proof of the origin of the Universe can be verified, although several theories have been formulated. The *soul* is the individual manifestation of the perpetual Universal Energy, which we call *spirit*. The spirit is the breath of life. "Breaking someone's spirit" is equivalent to producing psychological death, although the physical existence may continue. Even though recycling of the spirit cannot be demonstrated scientifically, it should be inferred as true. Universal Energy is the primal form of everything. It will never cease to exist. While it cannot be directly measured, this form of energy is just as real and true as traditionally accepted forms of energy, such as electrical and mechanical.

Although the manifestations of spiritual energy cannot be measured through conventional methods, its effects have been demonstrated numerous times. Spiritual development and maintenance requires dedicated concentration. As Buddhism teaches, being enlightened and going to Heaven require effort and faith (guided meditation and imagery). In the final analysis, concentration is the spiritual controller of humans. Praying is the most common form of focused concentration. Due to the busy life of materialistic societies, we have not yet learned to harness this energy in a repeatable way and use it properly. Though we have not yet found a reliable scientific proof, exceptions to the known rules of physics (miracles) often occur. These are brushed aside under various labels such as "unexplained mysteries" and "beyond reality."

Because the reality of an individual is his conscious manifestation of the ever-changing external existence, one can immediately infer the plausibility of a more complex life and Universe, which humans cannot sense with their physical sensors. While pacemakers, dialysis machines, and other artificial devices prolong our physical existence, no engineering marvel can channel spiritual energy. It can only be piped into the body through meditation and guided visualization. On the physical side, the Asians have used its manifestation for millennia to enhance the well being of the body as they transformed it into life energy for healing and longevity. This channeled energy was called "Prana" by the eastern yogi, "Lung-gom" by the Tibetan lamas, "Sakia-tundra" (also "Ki") by the Japanese Shinto priests, and "Chi" by the Taoist philosophers of China. The forms of Yoga, Chi Kung, Tai Chi, and other martial arts are only physical methods to keep the pathways through the body (meridians) open for Universal Energy to flow. It is the visualization attached to these physical forms that harnesses spiritual energy. This energy is the ever-present supreme engine of life. It has the physical effect of charging the nervous system of the body and the psychological effect of enhancing the emotional state of the individual. It is the energetic level at which man communicates with his own species, with other species, with nature, and with the Universe as a whole. After all, plants and animals do not respond in spoken language when they are spoken to.

The life energy of each living creature is the amount of spiritual energy retained from the energy of the dynamic Universe. Its intensity changes continuously. Birth and death rates on the planets modify the amplitude of its spectral components as spiritual energy is absorbed at birth and emanated at death. Because humans can cover a wide spectrum of emotions, they can vary the quantity of spiritual energy stored in accordance with their emotional state of being. Each "soul" is weakened by sadness or depression, or strengthened by states of excitement and joy. After all, it is just as exhausting to do physical labor, as it is to live in a state of psychological depression because both these actions cause energy depletion.

The earthly manifestation of the immortal energy that controls the existence of a living body is what world religions, literature, and the arts refer to as the *soul*. Early medieval thinkers defined the concept of eternity as the union of the human soul with the dynamic Universal intellect. The Aristotelian Jewish philosopher Moses Maimonides thought that after physical death only the souls of the righteous would survive. During the same time period, Averroës, a Spanish-Arab physician and philosopher, adhered to a similar idea. The notion that human souls are extensions of a single immortal soul is the probable seed of Giordano Bruno's concept of a collective cosmic mind, which follows Aristotle's definition of the universal soul. Carl Jung, the founder of analytical psychology, referred to a "collective unconscious," though he did not see it as a group consciousness to which the entire Universe is wired up, but as a collection of experiences built in time during evolution that we inherit in our genetic code. These primitive images pre-existent at birth are the "archetypes," and according to him are the roots of many of our tendencies. The new "Universal Energy Spectrum Theory" is based on the recycling of the spirit. It proposes that all souls are charged from a common energy source, but they gain their independence when their physical bodies are born. The Universal Energy Spectrum Theory uses spectral analysis to demonstrate the connection between personality characteristics and frequency components of the primordial energy of the Universe.

Being eternal energy, the soul is neither the intellect nor is it the instinct. It is the amount of spiritual energy retained by a living being. It is the spiritual energy that is seen in a living being's eyes. All life comes to Earth with a recycled soul. Living matter can take various forms of materialization. The human soul can be influenced through repetitions of actions and thoughts. As our species grows, we are reducing the populations of other species to satisfy our needs, thus modifying the Universal Energy Spectrum and the planetary environment. This action is directed by the human mind either as a result of conscious reasoning or subconscious programming, thus forming a very risky trend.

Just like any other form of energy, spiritual energy changes are propagated through waves. Waves can be thought of as connected local oscillations that take place within a medium. For example, audible sound waves are oscillations of local pressure through air that transfer acoustic energy from its source to our eardrum, making it vibrate. The amplitude of the waves carrying spiritual energy describes the depth of a personality characteristic, which is similar to the loudness of a continuous sound. Their frequency describes the type of personality characteristic (analytical, artistic, evil, etc.), which is similar to the tone of a sound. Spiritual energy is subject to the laws of conservation. At the beginning of the nineteenth century, Albert Einstein, in his theory of relativity proved that mass and energy are interchangeable. Thus, the law of conservation of mass discovered by Lavoisier, and the law of conservation of energy formulated later by Joule, were united. In the context of this modern theory of physics, the philosophical concept of "dualism," which separates soul from matter, cannot exist because the Universe and all of its components are only different manifestations of the Universal Energy, which can neither be created nor be destroyed. It can only be converted from one form to another. The law of conservation of energy, as a whole, gives the soul its *immortality* feature.

At the present level of evolution of the human species, mechanical work and physical endurance are the main characteristics of the body. The advanced ability to reason and imagery manipulation are those of the mind, and emotional being is the reflection of the energetic state of the soul. The union between the body (physical energy), the mind (thought energy), and the soul (spiritual energy) is the only way to define personality. The continuous interaction of these types of energy constitutes the dynamic personality of humans, animals, and all other life forms. All species, including humans, are born with initial spiritual energy. During their life, Moses, Jesus of Nazareth, Muhammad, Buddha, and Krishna could tune to various frequencies of the Universal Energy Spectrum, thus "feeling" the workings of the Universe. They were able to translate them into common human language, thus exhibiting prophetic abilities.

The physical body functions as an antenna. At birth, it receives energy from the Universal Energy Spectrum, and at death, it releases it back. The energy from the emitted waves, at death, returns to the Universal Energy Spectrum, thus magnifying the amplitude of various corresponding frequency components, as they resonate. The change in amplitude of a wave is produced by the additional energy provided, as new souls are released to the eternal Universal wave already existing in the field. The spiritual energy of each species has its own frequency range in the Universal Energy Spectrum. Physically, the life energy of a fetus while it develops in the womb is the result of the mother's ability to draw in energy from the Universe. Put more simply, when an individual of any species sheds its earthly body, it releases back to the Universe a packet of waves.

The type of life lived on the earthly plane (happy or sad, moral or immoral) controls the flow of energy. A spiritually uplifted life and positive earthly experiences will magnify the Universal Energy Spectrum. Any person whose soul sends back an energy-depleted packet, does so due to the impact of the negative experiences he had on Earth. Thus, the soul of a relatively happy and moral person, upon physical death, will enlarge selected frequency components of the Universal Energy Spectrum more than the soul of a chronically depressed individual. The spiritual energy emanated by each soul returns to the frequency band relegated to its species. Think of these spectral bands as strands in a rainbow. The lower strands are delegated for souls of lesser-evolved species, such as the worm or the ant. The strands continue to expand higher in proportion to the level of evolution of each species.

The highest strand is where human energy is released. Humans are assigned to the top strand as a species because of their ability to reason, interpret, and learn. We have much better tools with which to charge our souls than lesser-evolved species. All energy, upon the death of a living body, must be released back to the frequency band from where it originated. Thus, an ant's life energy can never ascend to the human strand and the human species can never descend to the ants' strand of energy. However, within each strand there is a bottom frequency and a top frequency. The waves corresponding to the frequency components contained within the spectral band of a species represent the personality characteristics of that species. Each being, depending on its soul, would revert to frequencies on its particular strand depending on how highly evolved that life form was.

Astrology ties the personality of each individual to the zodiac, as the spatial relationship between the planets and the Earth at the time of birth determines the polarity, the quality, and the element. Being heavily influenced by the ancient Eastern philosophy of Taoism, Jung believed that the date, the year, and even the season of birth are major determining factors of personality. According to the Universal Energy Spectrum Theory, the moment of birth determines the personality of a newborn, as the new soul is formed from the spiritual energy absorbed. When a child is born, it comes into the world predisposed to many characteristics such as artistic ability, processing and analysis capability, and disposition. The packet of energy absorbed from the Universal Energy Spectrum determines the personality characteristics at birth for all life creatures.

The Universal Energy Spectrum is complex and changes continuously. It contains waves of constant frequency, allowing the amplitude of each wave to constantly change. Each different frequency represents a different personality characteristic. The amplitude of a wave illustrates the amount of energy of its corresponding personality characteristic available at that selected frequency. At the moment of birth, the amplitude of each wave determines the maximum amount of energy the new soul can channel. The higher the amplitude, the more energy there is available, and thus there is more energy that can be absorbed. Although the entire spectrum of personality characteristics is available, the more energy absorbed at a certain frequency, the stronger the child will be in that area of ability. This "template," which is formed at birth only sets the upper limit of capability. A person may have the desire to play the piano. However, due to the limited energy absorbed at birth, he can never become another Beethoven. Also, one may have a tremendous capability to write and play music, but never develop it. Thus, his spiritual energy remains in a potential state, but is never activated.

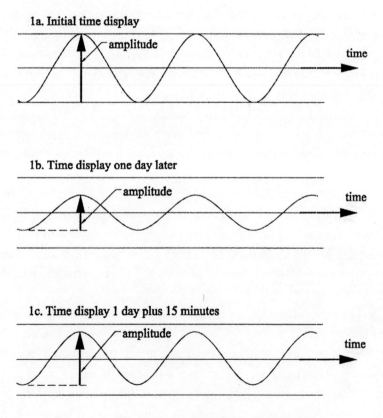

1a. Initial time display

1b. Time display one day later

1c. Time display 1 day plus 15 minutes

Figure 1. Amplitude change over time of a single wave

Let us look at the *example* of an artistic ability single wave shown in Figure 1a. The amplitude is one normalized unit. Twenty-four hours later, after people have been born and have died, the amplitude of that wave is completely different (Figure 1b). It has halved, which means that more Universal Energy was absorbed than was returned. Fifteen minutes later, after many births and deaths have occurred, the wave looks different yet again (Figure 1c). It appears that during that time, some of the energy in that wave has been restored. The amplitude of the wave keeps changing constantly as physical life appears and disappears in the Universe. Figure 2 illustrates the amplitude changes of three

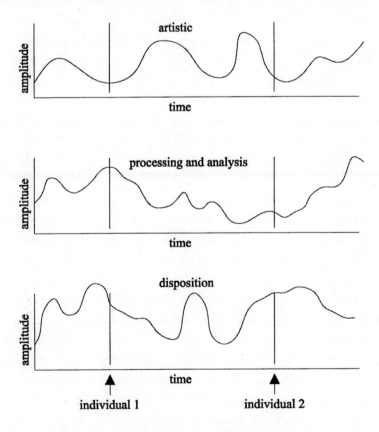

Figure 2. Historical change in amplitude for three waves

personality characteristics (energy per frequency component) that have occurred over a selected period of time. The personality characteristics of the waves presented are quite hilly and uneven, as the amount of energy extracted and absorbed constantly changes. Sample individual 1 was born with low artistic ability, high processing and analysis skills, and a pleasant disposition. This means that when this individual was born, the amplitude of the artistic ability wave was relatively low, thus a small amount of this spectral energy component was absorbed. The amplitude of the processing and analysis wave was high, and the amount of energy corresponding to the disposition characteristic wave was also high, thus a large amount of energy stored in these spectral components was absorbed. This is not the case of individual 2. His soul was charged with a low amount of energy corresponding to the artistic wave, with a low amount of energy corresponding to the processing and analysis wave, and a high amount of energy corresponding to the disposition characteristic wave.

As a newborn child is released from the womb, he comes into physical contact with the gravitational and the electromagnetic fields of the Earth for the first time, and charges his soul with Universal Energy. A new live "energy transformer" is created, a new person. The characteristics of the received wave packet create the tendencies that this new personality will have. The child is really a composite of selected characteristics from old souls with a new body. His energy has been used by former souls and was returned to the Universe at the time of physical death.

One of the most famous geniuses of the nineteenth century, Albert Einstein, was born to parents of average intelligence in Ulm (Germany) on March 14, 1879. A great believer in the order and perfection of the Universe, he redefined Physics when he set the foundation of one of the most important theories of life: nothing is absolute. Due to his distrust of dogmas and absolutism, Einstein found the secret of life by searching through the labyrinth of physical mysteries. His genius manifested in his desire not only to understand Creation, but also to determine what "God thought" when planning Universal perfection. Besides being the seed of modern physics, his Theory of Relativity will always remain a solid foundation for life, as it makes clear to the common man the concept that actions are always relative to definable circumstances. Einstein came into this world with a soul energized in the processing and analysis of information, which transcended science into other areas of human understanding. However, he had neither special physical nor artistic abilities. At birth, his soul definitely absorbed energy at the peak of the processing and analysis wave of the Universal Energy Spectrum. During his lifetime he developed it to its fullest potential.

The greatest musical genius of all time, Austrian composer Wolfgang Amadeus Mozart, was born in Salzburg on January 27, 1756. His ability could be recognized from the early age of six. During his short and unappreciated life of thirty-five years, he created more than six hundred musical works. His sublime music seems to have a cathartic effect on human beings. Psychologists use the "Mozart Effect" to temporarily enhance the analytical performance and raise the IQ of the listeners. However, his personality structure contained traces of manic-depression and a lack of adaptability to the society of his time. Although he was educated by his father who was a violinist and composer, his sophisticated techniques of creating magnificent music was an expression of the energy absorbed by his soul at the peak of the artistic wave of the Universal Energy Spectrum.

Adolph Hitler, the most powerful tyrant of the last century, was born in Braunau am Inn (Austria-Hungary) in 1889. Due to his desire to "purify" the human race and to dominate the world, his inconceivable evil deeds led to the slaughter of millions of Jews, Gypsies, and Russians. Although his father was a respected civil service worker who had high aspirations for his children, Hitler dropped out of high school and began his campaign of implementing one of the strongest dictatorships in world history. His evil nature, not shared by his other siblings, formed his soul by the energy absorbed at birth when it was charged at the bottom of the disposition wave of the Universal Energy Spectrum.

Newton, Beethoven, Picasso, Napoleon, and Shakespeare were born to parents of average ability. These are only a few examples that support the validity of the Universal Energy Spectrum Theory. It should be understood that human souls are not created equal. However, in the arena of life, man is given a choice to evolve or decline. The soul comes to Earth in a physical body. Man's mind and body can be used to activate the highest potential of his soul. Man's prejudice, greed, violence, and indifference or man's love, generosity, compassion, and empathy help determine how his personality and abilities evolve in this life. At any moment, the personality reflects the energetic state of the soul. The latent capability of the soul in any body, healthy or unhealthy, attractive or unattractive, can be awesome. It all depends on the spectral distribution of the Universal Energy at the time of birth.

Many human beings are endowed with strong ability characteristics, who given the opportunity could show their genius. Who knows how many children would be interested in light properties or have the ability to compose exquisite music? They will probably never have the opportunity to be another Einstein or Mozart. They have to work in sweatshops to be able to eat. They need the opportunity to expand their personality characteristics hidden in their souls. As the incandescent filament of the light bulb is the means by which to change a flow of electrons in visible photons, the catalysts for energizing ability characteristics to find the truth of genius are human living conditions, knowledge, unequivocal faith in continuous success, understanding by society, and relentless persistence.

Learning and personal experience can increase the soul's energetic level within the limit of the initial energetic template. The mind functions as a controller. From time to time, the connection between the soul and the Universal Energy Spectrum is disrupted, and more than one template is formed for the same soul. This materializes in "altered states of consciousness" such as multiple personalities within the same person, which is a temporary shift between the templates. Although such spectral transfer is characteristic to individuals with highly developed spiritual abilities, their souls always revert to their initial frequency spectrum. Positive affirmations and guided meditation are the main methods by which to enrich the soul through earthly life. Because doubtless affirmation and deep meditation require clearing of the conscious mind, they create an unbiased impression in the subconscious mind, thus acting directly on the soul. Creating positively charged images and movies that are programmed and run repetitively by the subconscious mind is the most effective means by which to mold the soul. Depression is a temporary depletion of the soul, while joy is a temporary charging of it. The soul's energy can be modified by beliefs and attitudes. The health of the body is also a contributing factor to the energetic level of the soul.

Animals also have an individual soul. Due to their lack of articulate language animals are unable to cross into the frequency band assigned to humans within the Universal Energy Spectrum. Unlike animals that live in the wild, pets have a frequency-shifted soul. Perhaps this is due to their constant interaction with human souls. They "borrow" from our soul's higher energies (love), or from some of our soul's less desirable energy (hate, violence). Thus, the pet takes on the persona of his owner. If a pet is energetic, happy, and playful, that is the direct result of his owner's care. If a pet is distant, frightened, or violent, this too can be attributed to the owner's soul-to-soul contact with his pet. Jungle animals have less developed souls, as they are never exposed to humans' souls, which can so greatly influence them. Jungle animals live mainly by instinct. They are too involved in meeting their primitive needs, such as protecting themselves and finding food. They never have the opportunity to exchange energy with people.

When you leave your human body, your soul returns to its original creator, the Universal Energy Spectrum – the rainbow. We have the responsibility when we leave our human body, to send back a fully charged soul. Being the best part of what we were, parts of this soul may be inherited by another human body, and make its contribution to this world. If a soul is depleted, the bodies, which inherit this soul or parts of it, will be at a distinct disadvantage. When an individual leads an unhappy life, some East European cultures believe that he is paying for the wrong doings of others who have died. This may be true if the timing of the soul formation of this individual is poor due to its unfortunate aligning of the personality characteristic waves. In this particular case, the result would be similar to the theory of "karma," where the retribution of one's actions during his lifetime takes place during a following life.

Only if humans continue to develop the positive characteristics of their personalities can mankind advance. If we continue to send back energy deficient souls, it will take humanity eons of time to achieve enlightenment. We will continue to grow monsters and be haunted by menacing gangs, murderers, and abusers. Humanity will never reach the pinnacle of success, which would be a world full of earthly angels. The recycling of the soul cannot be proven through present scientific capabilities. Even if you adhere to Nietzsche's thought that "many things are not believed because their explanation is not believed," and have doubts about the continuity of the spirit in spite of the enormous evidence reported by medical professionals, psychologists, or by people who have achieved altered states of consciousness, it seems reasonable for all humans to make every effort to prolong the last stretch on the journey to perfection. This is the reason!

2

Knowledge

Our capacity to acquire and store knowledge is our most precious possession. It is the key by which to obtain eternal satisfaction, which is our human legacy. It is more valuable than our wealth, possessions, or power. When we are learning we become one with our destiny, that of our evolutionary development. Knowledge should be the tool by which we can heal our ignorance. It appears that the more knowledge humans acquire, the more mired in fear, doubt, and hostility they become. Knowledge should be a powerful tool used to create peace, love, and harmony and by which to avoid a planetary crisis.

Knowledge enables us to continuously adapt to new realities. Webster's New World Dictionary and Thesaurus defines knowledge as, "all that has been perceived by the mind." The theory of knowledge and truth is the subject of epistemology. The most primitive knowledge is by acquaintance as man learns through his senses. The articulate and the scientific knowledge are descriptive or propositional. There is a major difference between experience and propositional knowledge. Experience is a philosophical concept encompassing everything that man senses in life from physical phenomena to emotions. Propositional knowledge is the representation of various experiences. While

21

experiences are the components of life, propositional knowledge is a description of life's experiences. Today's computers can store large amounts of information acquired from the experiences of many people. At this level the information can be qualified as objective knowledge. Everyone can adopt it. The experience of reality is subjective and particular to one's own experience. Wisdom is created through understanding and reflection. It is the power to reason that will always make humans the owners of computers and not the other way around. According to the Bhagavad Gita, "…forgiveness, simplicity, purity, steadfastness, self-control is declared to be wisdom," and "what is opposed to this is ignorance." Wisdom includes facts, information, concepts, and all principles accumulated by mankind. It appears "normal" to the ordinary man to be utterly convinced of the sufficiency of his knowledge because it guides him successfully through his current stage of life. Unfortunately, time makes yesterday's knowledge insufficient for today's needs, and as the Universe allows man to understand some of its secrets, human curiosity keeps him looking for new ones. The human mind is evolving at a rapid pace. Physically we are not much different than our ancestors who lived more than 10,000 years ago. However, with the emergence of conscious awareness we are able to direct our future. The slow process of adaptation and trial and error no longer binds us. We are able to learn from past generations and to make informed decisions about the world we inhabit.

In the final analysis, knowledge is the result of a chain of events beginning at discovery and ending with validation. Being convinced of the certainty of the perceived reality through his senses, and being conditioned to hold true his own preconceived ideas, man validates all new information acquired, either through observation or through communication, by filtering it through his pre-existing knowledge. He sorts his new information by importance and quality, and absorbs it into his knowledge bank, thus enriching his filtering capability for the future acquisition of knowledge. As doubt is removed through repetition, man's bank of knowledge continuously grows, thus making life a never-ending process of learning. Based on this continuous process of education, reason, and individual experience, man builds wisdom. Man needs to understand that merely collecting facts in his brain only makes his mind a receptacle for information. He needs wisdom to help use this knowledge intelligently, and for the benefit of all mankind. "The work will teach you how to do it," says an Estonian proverb. Solving the problems of life, and trying to find ways to survive during adversity builds man's character, and increases his wisdom.

The level of knowledge at a given point in history dictates the quality of life. At the beginning of the nineteenth century, Martin Van Buren reported to President Andrew Jackson that railroad carriages were being pulled by steam engines at breakneck speeds of fifteen miles per hour, which at that time would be inconceivable even to God. We already have supersonic commercial flights over the Atlantic Ocean, and we have exceeded the speed of sound many times over in aircraft speed. This progress in sciences and technology will continue to take place at a much faster rate as the power of computers minimizes the time required for routine research jobs. There is no doubt that cancer, the killer disease of today, will be treated as easily as a mild infection by future generations. This progress in science is established upon our natural thirst for knowledge. Science cannot be content with the shallow, apparent, and transparent explanation of facts. Sciences such as chemistry, physics, biology, and medicine investigate what appears to be obvious or convenient in order to establish its legitimacy. In this way, science can help the common man to understand his world, and to live a longer, more satisfying life.

Since the time Adam and Eve tasted the forbidden fruit from the Tree of Knowledge, man has never stopped his search for truth and thirst for knowledge. "The greater our knowledge increases, the more our ignorance unfolds," said President Kennedy. Unfortunately, there will always be people in positions of power, who will mistakenly try to retard the inborn desire to transform imagination into reality. After all, Napoleon chuckled at Fulton's idea to use steam power for ship transportation instead of wind sails. In spite of the fact that "great spirits always encountered violent opposition from mediocre minds" *(Albert Einstein),* the ability of human beings to learn, and use logic will continue to allow the human race to conquer new frontiers in science and humanities, and to always dominate the animal kingdom.

It is of immediate concern that human knowledge begins to advance in a non-compartmentalized fashion, matching the completeness of the Universal design. On humanity's last stretch to God, man must forever renounce his arrogance of priding himself a superior species, and focus his attention on the preservation of his oneness with nature and the Universe. Knowledge is now available to everyone interested in growing intellectually. Today, when separatism is increasing due to the loss of tolerance under tyrannical governments, knowledge can be misused. One should always remember that two "small" nuclear bombs ended the Second World War in the Far East with very regrettable consequences, and the atomic weapons available today can destroy our planet, and no one will remain to measure its effects.

The bodies of all animated beings developed instinctual knowledge necessary for existence through the use of their senses, which are used to probe the surrounding environment. Hot, cold, light, and dark are learned through physical experience. It is through our bodies that our species can continue its existence. The human mind with its capability to reason, in conjunction with its available long-term storage capacity of the memory, enables man to learn throughout life into old age. The use of articulate language enables each generation to leave its knowledge to posterity, thus allowing the continuous progress of humanity. All beings experience consciousness. Animals can only experience consciousness of the present moment, thus having a limited awareness of their world. The difference between humans and animals is that we have an insightful consciousness. The reflective nature of our consciousness enables us to be aware of our existence and be conscious that we are aware. Language enables us to use imagination, an advantage that animals don't have.

Man evolved by confronting challenges and solving problems throughout history. Each peril helped him to forge a smarter brain and a better body. In particular, the power to reason, knowledge, and creativity continued to grow. Evolution shows that Homo Sapiens, with their superior brains and linguistic abilities, survived and flourished while the less mentally evolved Neanderthal man and Homo Erectus became extinct. Throughout early history, our bodies continually changed to adapt to the demands of unique environments and diets.

The mind holds man a prisoner. He needs to escape from this state of entrapment of rigid thoughts and emotions by realizing that making errors in judgment, and being deceived by appearances can put him into a state of confusion. The mind guides his actions, controls his thoughts, and molds his perception of the world. The mind guards man's identity and acts as a sieve through which he can filter thoughts and experiences and interpret them. Unfortunately, man's mind is cluttered with negativities, selfishness, and prejudices. These were learned at a very early age and continuously reinforced. Thus, the mind now accepts them as truth. New learning therefore, becomes difficult, due to the constant interpretation of each new piece of information and coloring it with individual prejudices. When man realizes how trapped he is through his thoughts, interpretations, desires, and hatred, he can resolve to change. It is well known that "success is measured by one's willingness to keep trying" *(Anonymous)*. Knowledge gives man the power of choice. He needs to be the director of his mind.

Throughout history there have been periods where man slaughtered one another in the name of religion. Wars were fought based on hatred, greed, jealousy, and power. In the last century, due to his creativity and increased knowledge, man has been able to develop automatic weapons and weapons of mass destruction. It was not much more than fifty years ago when more than eleven million people were slaughtered for the reason of creating a perfect race. Of course, even during man's darkest hours, there were always enlightened individuals. Knowledge gave them the power to create an emotional state that allowed them to develop a clear view of the solution through the clouded madness of the crowds. However, knowledge used incorrectly, without compassion, can increase man's capability for evil. It must be used consciously to supplant feelings of hatred, revenge, and jealousy with feelings of altruism, compassion, and responsibility.

Man is also conscious of external perceptions, the things and events outside of himself and the sensations of his body and how they feel. It is his mind, which interprets events and experiences in his world; it acts both as a lens and a guide, constantly evaluating, interpreting, judging, and fabricating. It is due to this that two people can experience the same event quite differently depending on the thoughts and interpretations of their minds. Unfortunately, individual minds are tainted with neurotic thoughts, self-blame, guilt, negativities, and selfishness. These thoughts cloud the experience of their world. We are in a prison of insecurity and loneliness. Each human being must learn to observe, and consciously monitor his thoughts, and replace discouraging and destructive ones with those of peace, love, and joy. Only by controlling our thoughts and making them healthy, positive, and compassionate, will Universal harmony prevail.

Man has made more technological progress in the past two hundred years than in the previous million. Today, man's power to reason and his innovative capacity continue to develop at a spectacular rate. With sophisticated equipment and machinery, man no longer needs to exercise his body beyond what is considered healthy. We no longer have to depend on our arms and legs to run, hunt, and defend ourselves. As man evolved, he traded physical ability for mental capability. With knowledge, we will continue to evolve and develop our mental capacity. Studies show that as the human body ages, the brain loses very little function. We are capable of creating and learning throughout our entire life. The brain, like any other muscle, needs to be exercised to remain strong. The mind must be preserved and trained to continually gain wisdom and enrich the soul.

Within the Hebrew mysticism of the Kabbalah, the top triad of the Tree of Life, which is a representation of Creation, is composed of three divine manifestations: Keter (God's crown), the Hochma (Wisdom emanated by the Infinite), and Binah (Understanding and connecting with the lower worlds). The guiding principle of the Kabbalah is the elevation of life through ten divine manifestations of existence. It must be noted that Wisdom and Understanding act as a base for the crown of God. They form the last bridge toward fusion with the Infinite. The Kabbalists believe in the duality of sin and redemption. According to their teachings, "good" must be defined through knowledge. Any other definition cannot lead to the correct meaning of "real goodness," and will always be biased by the temporal and cultural tendencies of society. The mind can be programmed to want good things. Correct training is necessary to align the body with the mind. Emotions, when driven by knowledge, can initiate change. All intellectual growth originates in the mind, but unless our emotions agree, we will not follow through with our ideas.

Knowledge can shape our destiny by tuning man's wishes with the Universal order, and with its goals. Unfortunately, very few of us ever ask ourselves what our destiny is. Our free will allows us to choose a part of our destiny. The other part of our destiny is determined the day we are born. At that time, we are given our birth date, time in history, birth family, country, and our talents and limitations. We are privy to the problems and advantages of that time. Of course, it is ideal to be born in a time of peace, to happily married and thoughtful parents who are able to afford us many opportunities. Our challenge from the Universe might be to create our destiny, in spite of obstacles. Realistic goals, coupled with knowledge, guides man toward his destiny. Our biggest fear as human beings is to have lived a life devoid of meaning. It is this fear, which drives us towards opportunities to grow and to find out on an individual level what we deem to be important.

Wisdom is achieved through the accumulation of knowledge and the human capacity to reason. The few people who could afford the time to study, understand, and reflect have monopolized it. Today, when the dissipation of information is overwhelming, man must strive to become wise in order to succeed in a more complex life. "The words of wise men are heard in quiet more than the cry of him that ruleth among fools" *(Ecclesiastes 9:17)*.

While procreation is common to all natural species, gaining wisdom and building spiritual strength is characteristic only to humans. Since the time of the Old Testament, it has been acknowledged that gaining wisdom takes time, and that a "multitude of years should teach wisdom" *(Job 32:7)*. While knowledge can be transferred at will either through oral or written communication, wisdom cannot be bought or sold. This is why the Chinese say, "learning is a treasure which accompanies its owner everywhere." Many have lost their wealth, but nobody can lose his knowledge and his wisdom. This guaranteed ownership makes it a most precious commodity.

Before becoming king, young Solomon, the son of David and Bathsheba, asked God in his dream for wisdom. Because he did not ask for wealth or an extended life, God gave him "a wise and understanding heart; so that there was none like thee before thee" *(Kings 3:12)*. His wisdom became proverbial through the story of his judgment of two prostitutes, each claiming to be the mother of the same newborn child. By simulating an attempt to cut the child in two pieces and give each woman her half, he produced the necessary proof required for a correct verdict. He granted custody of the child to the woman who accepted to give her child up just to save his life. The entire kingdom was deeply impressed by his wisdom and his sense of justice. His insight resonated throughout other lands. When Queen Sheba came to visit, she tested him, and was thoroughly impressed with his answers to her enigmatic questions. For King Solomon, wisdom shines brightly forever. "The true beginning of Wisdom is the desire to learn..., and the desire for wisdom leads to kingly stature" *(Apocrypha; Wisdom of Solomon 6:18-21)*. It is this never-ending process of learning, which makes man wise as his life experiences guide him along the path of enlightenment. "Give instruction to a wise man, and he will be yet wiser; teach a just man, and he will increase in learning" *(Proverbs 9:9).* As a general rule, the wise man will always be ready to learn and elevate his level of knowledge. Regrettably, the reverse of this rule can be disastrous. It manifests as the inability of the ignorant that not only refuse to learn, but live and die convinced that they knew it all. In positions of power, they become a real danger to society, as they will not adapt to a life of continuous learning, which is necessary to attain oneness with the perfect Universe. Dire thoughts lead to "unfortunate" circumstances for all of us. Is this what the story of Genesis teaches when "God saw that the wickedness of man was great in the Earth, and that every imagination of the thoughts of his heart was only evil continually" *(Genesis 6:5)*?

The understanding of what billions of negative thought waves can do should revolutionize our thinking. All harmful thinking would stop, if we could grasp the seriousness of what we might be causing to others and to ourselves. Thoughts, being energy, shoot out from our mind and mix with billions of other thoughts. They can do several things. Being transmitted as waves, they can refract, hit their target, or reflect back to the thinker. In their interaction, they can change their content and direction. Few of us are able to channel universal energy to the desired target. Therefore, these thoughts may bounce around randomly, and no one can predict where or on whom they will land.

There are a myriad of possible scenarios, which can follow an evil thought. Let's examine only a few. If your thought was, "I wish I were dead," this energy would be emanated into the Universe. Soon after this thought you would meet with a situation or accident in which you would lose your physical life. This is the least probable scenario because it is the rare individual who can focus his thought energy so perfectly. Another possible scenario would be that somewhere, someone on the planet would die due to this thought wave. The next possibility would be that this negative thought would interfere with a positive thought and be neutralized. A more frightening scenario would be that this thought wave would interfere with a multitude of other negative thoughts and in so doing gain tremendous momentum. This could result in cataclysmic disasters such as deaths, fires, accidents, and the formation of hate groups. It is impossible to predict the outcome of such a phenomenon. Another example might be that your thought was, "I hate my neighbor. I wish he would lose his job." There is a small possibility that this would happen. Perhaps you would lose *your* job due to this thought wave reflecting back to you. Another possibility would be that someone else on the planet would become unemployed due to such a thought wave. Hopefully, this thought wave would be neutralized and no harm would be done.

Let's now see what might happen due to a positive thought. Suppose your thought was, "I wish my friend would get well." The best scenario would be that your friend would recover. Both of you would be extremely fortunate if you were able to hit your target. However, if you could collect a group of people to "wish your friend well," your collective thoughts would have much more power than a single thought. Another auspicious situation would be that someone, somewhere, would get well. The worst possible scenario would be that a negative thought wave would neutralize your positive thought wave and nothing would happen. Most significant is that this positive energy could *never* harm anyone. All of humanity would benefit from a much-needed positive shift in their thinking.

It is only wisdom, which will help the human species to survive in this world perceived as "random." A part of wisdom is adaptation. Animals have been doing it since the beginning of time. Humans have become inept at this. It is difficult to accept, change, and navigate around uncertain circumstances. Change requires effort and risk. Aside from changing our clothes with the changing seasons, we don't want to adapt. When the expected outcome does not materialize, we feel victimized, and we are unable to cope. Man needs to understand that it is his perception of circumstances that define his view of life, not the circumstances themselves. "Man is made by his belief. As he believes, so he is" *(Bhagavad Gita)*. It is in this context that knowledge and his ability to reason must become his guiding light, not his emotions. It is reason, not irrational passion that will finally prevail.

Adapting does not mean giving up. On the contrary, adapting means trying again or seeking a different path. How is it that individuals faced with extraordinary difficulties in their lives manage to prevail? How is it that many times, severely disabled people have a better attitude than those of us with mundane problems that we think are important, but pale in comparison to theirs? How is it that the severely handicapped often lead happier lives than those who are not? The answer is simple: these people are able to adapt. They realize the power within them. They do not see an unleveled playing field. They follow the guiding light of their souls. They realize that their body may be impaired or their intellect might be damaged. However, these people are able to adapt to their situation even with what may seem to us hideous circumstances. We would think that it would be easier for those without handicaps to adapt, but it is not. We have created other handicaps such as greed, envy, power, and prestige. Because of these self-created dilemmas and the power of random thoughts, we do not have complete control over our circumstances. Strong adaptive skills, coupled with reason and knowledge, are the keys to a happy and fulfilled life.

The wise man knows that he needs to use his wisdom, ability to reason, intelligence, and intuition. With these abilities he will then make the best decision he can make at any time. When he does not use these abilities, he knows there is a good chance that he will make a mistake. The outcome that he hoped for, but did not plan for, may not materialize. If the Universe does not smile upon him with what he wanted, he must accept graciously what comes his way and make the best of the situation. He must adapt to this new set of circumstances (although painful) and learn from the experience. However, if he feels he did his best, and he did not get the expected outcome, this unhappy circumstance was probably the result of a negative thought wave. He intuitively understands that it is not completely his fault, and seeks a new outcome or another route by which to get what he desires. The wise man not only looks for lessons in the unexpected, but also for new challenges, even during what some might label a failure. The wise man knows that being attached to any one outcome is a dangerous and narrow view. He makes the best decision he can and then holds his breath. He knows that he is in the middle of the movie, and expectantly waits to see the path the Universe wants him to follow. The wise man knows there is no such thing as a bad experience. He replaces the words "if only" with "next time." The wise man is not necessarily the one with the highest IQ. He is not always the one with the most education or the richest. He is the one who can easily adapt. This is a well-adjusted individual.

It is a well-known fact that if any animal is unable to adapt to its environment, it will die. For humans, the inability to adapt leads people to terrorism and to holy wars. If we as a species refuse to adjust our attitudes to our circumstances, and if we refuse to accept or to find another path when needed, we too will suffer physically and psychologically. During our earthly life, the Universe forces us to adapt, learn, and acquire wisdom. It is up to us to consciously develop an inquiring mind, and make the effort needed to learn from our experiences and from the experiences of others. "Only take heed to thyself, and keep thy soul diligently, lest thou forget the things which thine eyes have seen" *(Deuteronomy 4:9)*.

In primitive times, many people survived with few material possessions. However, these societies were rich in culture, beliefs, and values. Today we view this as an archaic way of life and have supplanted these values with our modern values: those of wealth, prestige, and power. If we could study the nature of despair throughout history, perhaps we would find that the cause of human suffering hasn't changed. While we would wonder at the origin of science, medicine, religion, and philosophy, we would be astounded by the lack of development in the humanistic realm. We seem still to be in the infancy stage of discovery as to how to halt our human suffering.

Today, western society is the inheritor of tremendous material wealth and convenience. This unrealistic standard is unobtainable for many societies around the globe. The gap between the wealthy nations with an abundance of opportunity and those whose opportunity is severely limited continues to widen. This polarization in economic and social development instills anger and vengeance in the less fortunate nations. While the richer nations enjoy material wealth, superior health-care, and individual freedom, our less fortunate neighbors struggle for basic survival. It would seem that it is not only the moral responsibility, but it should also become the deliberate intent of the wealthy to educate the less fortunate, thus giving them a chance for a better life. While mortality rates are being reduced in economically advanced countries through the continuous development of life sciences, the birth rate in most underdeveloped countries is skyrocketing. Although it may appear to be a localized issue, the population explosion is one of our most ardent global concerns. Constant dissipation of knowledge around the globe is the only method by which to manage the birth rate. A steady decrease in the human birth rate, which is out of control in underdeveloped countries, is the only effective way to prevent the destruction of humankind through overpopulation.

We are global citizens. We hold enormous potential to knowingly affect other species, our environment, and the fate of all humankind. We can communicate to others information about our thoughts, desires, emotions, and dreams. We can make informed and ethical choices regarding our future. We have evolved from primitive cavemen to men who can walk on the moon. Developed nations have evolved from farming societies to leaders in information and technology. We are transferring knowledge through telecommunications and information processing. The human mind is evolving at a rapid pace. With conscious awareness and correct use of reason, we are better able to control our destiny. We are able to learn from past generations, and to make informed decisions about the world we inhabit.

Evolution cannot continue unless we solve our global problems. The change will not only need to be in the thinking realm, but in the human realm of the heart. Our mental set must change from one of self-concern to one of global concern. We must forego our dominant need for taking care of only our loved ones and ourselves, and replace it with one that is benevolent and globally conscious. Being knowledge-able is a magnificent way to travel on the last stretch to God.

3

Truth

The earthly truth does not have a unique definition. Due to its relative nature, many philosophical theories of truth have been developed throughout history. Scientists use the *pragmatic* definition of truth in their investigations. They establish the truthfulness of a concept by subjecting it to tests, which are designed according to a preexisting theory. According to Einstein, "truth is what stands the test of experience." Theologicians consider a proposition to be true if it agrees with their beliefs. Blaise Pascal believed that truth couldn't be known by reason only, "but also by the heart." Although the pragmatic definition may not be complete, it does offer the satisfaction of making reality more predictable. The *correspondence* definition is also used to describe the earthly truth. It is accepted that a proposition is true if it corresponds to one or more concurring facts. The more conclusive the facts, the closer one can get to this truth. Both definitions of truth are intertwined in the legal systems of the West, when man judges his peers. The absolute truth represents perfection for the scientist, and it defines the image of God for the theologician. Because nothing can exist and not exist at the same time, truth can be viewed as the opposite of falsehood. As supporting evidence is analyzed, in the final analysis, it is human intelligence and ethics, which are used to deduce and defend the earthly truth. Although never attainable by man, the intrinsic human desire to approach the absolute truth drives mankind forward.

At this time in history, the very existence of the planet is at risk. Due to the ever-growing tendency toward dishonest diplomacy, irrational egomania, greed, and the loss of value for human life, every member of a society must understand that the use of lying, dishonesty, and pre-meditated deception is more dangerous now than ever. It not only ruins everyone's gift of life, it also hurts mankind, and through the leverage of technology, it is slowly destroying our world. Only the truth can elevate man to his final destination of happiness, and prolong his stay on the planet Earth. Daily breakthroughs in science are bring-ing us closer to perfection in the physical realm of life. However, because the human justice system and the ethical value system are incompatible, an urgent look inward is required to recapture the con-cept of truth, thus attempting to regain the joy of living within a fragile human community. Every effort has to be made to eradicate the most dangerous predicament of our time: the proliferation of lying at all lev-els of human existence.

Life today is fraught with endless conflicts. Decisions are made con-tinuously at all levels of the world community from personal choices to declarations of war. At the current level of social progress, we have attained the highest degree of competition and the most sophisticated means of communication ever imaginable. Any possible method is being used to convince man that pushing to get ahead and always striv-ing toward material abundance is the guaranteed road to happiness. The media, with it's multitude of distribution channels, including tab-loids, published material, radio and television broadcasting, and flash-ing banners on various web sites is dissipating information in a most timely manner. At the click of a button, a multitude of choices are made based on the information received. In our unnecessary striving toward material gain, deceiving infomercials and misleading marketing techniques catch us at times when we are relaxed and most open to suggestion. The emotions created through repetition have a hypnotic effect on our mind and they can poison our soul. When our logic is defeated by a marketing method designed to target a certain weakness, the advertised product or service appears as a necessity of life. We become confused by the conflicting emotions created by the misleading images and finally, the mind asks the body to do regretful acts.

Life is complicated and it is inevitable that tough choices need to be made. We need criteria by which we can make both small choices and decisions of major proportions. *Unless a life hangs in the balance*, we need always to be truthful regardless of the outcome. History has recorded many cases when authority was disobeyed, when lying was the only way to save life. How can we forget what God told Moses? "Thou shalt no go up and down as a talebearer among thy people: neither shalt thou stand against the blood of thy neighbor" *(Leviticus 19:16)*. Could this be viewed as a double standard? Wasn't lying one of the ways used by Gentiles to save the lives of many European Jews during the Nazi era? Can it stand flawlessly together with the Commandment: "Though shalt not bear false witness against thy neighbor" *(Exodus 20:16)?* Contrary to a superficial analysis, it can. When the "righteous ones" risked their own lives to shield the lives of other innocent human beings, they raised themselves to the level of absolute truth, which implies the genuine protection of the most brilliant work crafted by the Universe, the human life. In the third millennium, when peace cannot be secured around the globe, and it is not easy to envision a perfect Universe, these two biblical verses must actually complement each other. People must live in peace with their neighbors, and be truthful to each other. In today's imperfect world of exploding population and failing diplomacy, adhering unconditionally to moral life principles is the only ethical personal choice. If mankind can be saved from destruction, man must always aspire to fuse with the absolute truth. Neither the courts of law, nor the envoys of the United Nations Organization can save humanity, only the truth will.

Although philosophers try to find ways to objectively describe the absolute truth, anything that can be said about it is untrue, because any description would try to place ethical limits on objectivity. The absolute truth does not depend on any statement. It is the perfection and the pure essence of life. Absolute truth can be viewed as the sacred quest of all human beings toward the demolition of the walls of self-imposed spiritual limitations. All religions adhere to similar characterizations of the absolute truth. According to the Old Testament, absolute truth is a representation of God. It is revealed by its everlasting validity, reliability, and dependability, which are guaranteed by the perfection of the divine. According to a Jewish midrash (a rabbinic commentary on the Bible), there are four classes of people who will never see the face of the *Shechinah* (the image of God): the mockers, the hypocrites, the slanderers, and the liars. The New Testament teaches dedication to the absolute truth, which constitutes the bond of humanity and the fellowship of all human beings. It presents the absolute truth as the basis for ideal freedom. Ananias and his wife Sapphira, tried to deceive the apostle Peter by withholding money they voluntarily pledged to a collection for an early Christian community. This premeditated deception brought death to both of them. They could not face their sin of lying, not only "unto men, but onto God" *(Acts 5:6)*. This vivid scene of self-inflicted punishment for the sinful act of lying shows unequivocally the position of Christianity regarding hypocrisy and dishonesty. The Sufi martyr al-Husain ibn Mansur al-Hallaj had been accused of heresy and executed at the end of the first millennium because of his belief which he stated publicly: "Ana al Haqq" ("I am the Truth"). The ideological doctrine that a man can proclaim himself the human incarnation of the absolute truth, the synonym for God, was unacceptable to the Caliph of Baghdad. One of the ethical directions given in the "Eightfold Path" by Buddhist philosophy to attain the blissful state of "nirvana" is "right speech," which implies telling the truth, being compassionate, offering encouragement, and being helpful. Although condemned by Buddha more than two and a half millennia ago, lying has become an important part of daily living.

Today, many people embrace the idea of the "situational ethics" system of thought. It is based on the concept that prohibition against lying and the assertion of truth are valid ethical concepts, thus the proper choice becomes a matter of a personal view of right and wrong action. It is socially accepted that being human implies being subjective. As the Universe gives each of us a certain amount of time between birth and death to manage our existence, no one has the right to disturb anyone else's time on Earth through dishonesty and lying. It is worth stressing again that *unless life is in danger*, each "justified" half-truth can, and in most cases will, hurt someone else. One must always use his ability to reason to find a truthful path, and not justify deception by intentionally concealing the truth. Although we can strive to find our "subjective truth," objective sincerity is always expected. Honesty must remain the preferred way of life.

Let us examine how unknowingly, and with the best of intentions, deceptions are generated. These are falsities, which we deem so insignificant, so trivial, that they are not even noticed. These are lies, which do no apparent harm, but are part of the social amenities of our society. They are built into our language and are used out of habitual politeness. Phrases such as, "How do you do?" or "How are you?" are used daily. After all, it is doubtful that the salesman who calls from the other end of the country is really interested in our health problems, our marital difficulties, and the discord we may have with our children. He just wants to sell something. I doubt that even acquaintances who we work with are really interested in how we are. A simple "Good afternoon" or "Hello" would be sufficient. If this practice becomes a habit, then when someone inquires how we are, we would realize that they are genuinely concerned and interested. These minor deceptions seem inconsequential. They appear to have no negative effect on anyone. However, they are not the genuine truth. They silently set the stage for more significant lies.

The psychological basis for deceit is the desire of one man's mind to assume control over another man's soul. Since the soul mirrors the absolute truth, even when we justify an insignificant lie, we are corrupting our consciousness by distorting the meaning of truth. In many instances, the earthly truth is only an illusion filtered through the historical and cultural structure of the language. Pragmatically, the truth or the lie is partly defined by the mind and partly by the belief. For the Western materialistic society, which cannot distinguish between reality and television, finding an acceptable rationalization for the truth is practically impossible. Whose reality is true? Is it the one presented on the screen or the one experienced by the viewer? Is it the one on the tongue or the one in the heart?

A group of "inconsequential" lies are the ones we've labeled "white lies." These are small lies used with the best of intentions, to avoid hurting someone else's feelings. Many times they flatter someone or put a more optimistic face on an otherwise distressing situation. These small deceptions may seem insignificant to the liar, but may be viewed differently by the one being deceived. After all, who really wants to get a dishonest compliment about a haircut or suit? If we are unsure about our attire or appearance, we would appreciate a kind, but honest appraisal. From the birth of a child, when white lies are commonly used to delight the new parents, to the eulogy of the dead, when the same technique is used to comfort the survivors, this petty hypocrisy is invading our daily lives. Always, a more appropriate policy would be to not volunteer information unless asked, and then tell the kindest truth. Initially, it may be unpleasant, but the other person will appreciate it. Our soul pays heavily when we lie. Dishonesty harms everyone. It may appear kind to use a white lie to make a depressing situation seem less hopeless. However, are we really doing a favor or a disservice by deceiving someone? This person does not need our sympathy. He needs our intelligence and our ability to reason. He needs our help. He needs an honest opinion and constructive suggestions as to how to improve or adapt to the situation. Just imagine the devastating effect a lie can have in the long run.

White lies are sometimes told out of friendship or loyalty. Evaluations for students, employees, or colleagues must be written honestly. Dishonest recommendations can have significant consequences to the candidate whose reviewer wrote a candid appraisal of his abilities. They will confuse the employer. He may accept a candidate who is less qualified than required for that position. Why not give a truthful recommendation? Why sign a worthless diploma? Why not give an honest interview? It is this disregard for truth, which helps many people reach commanding positions in the work place or in society. Helping a dishonest "one" will invariably result in punishing the honest "many." Ugly divorces, unending labor and management disputes, and bloody wars are rooted in the lack of truth. Integrity, honesty, and respect for our fellow man will always be rewarded by trust and personal satisfaction.

The dishonesties and exaggerations used in gossip are usually classified as white lies. An Irish proverb says that when participating in gossip, one "brings a tale and takes two away." Of course, this can only be explained by the complete neglect of one's power to reason and by the dubious use of one's intelligence. How can we elevate our soul and anyone else's if we participate in slander? There is no justification for gossip, as its outcome can be disastrous. The Zen maxim saying, "when one person tells a lie, countless others tell it as a truth" can be considered a comprehensive description of the danger of gossip. It shows how wrong it is to qualify gossip and white lies as trivial and harmless. How can we ever serve the truth with a lie? No matter what the justification for lying is, there is always harm to the liar himself, to the one who was deceived, and to society as a whole. An individual who is caught lying, knowingly or unknowingly, places his integrity at risk forever. Lies take their toll on intimacy and honesty. This is often done subtly, unconsciously, until the individual feels a deep ache in his soul due to his lack of personal integrity. Any husband or wife who has been deceived will attest to the fact that once having been lied to, they are often unable to trust their spouses again.

Lies used for getting out of major difficulties and even minor conflicts must be avoided. Our ability to reason, and our acquired wisdom should be used to devise appropriate truthful alternatives to diffuse such situations. Excusing a wrongdoing with another lie will never lead to the truth. Minimizing the consequences through a truthful apology is always a better way. Because the truth satisfies a questioning mind, when we fulfill our duty to ourselves and to others by telling the truth as diplomatically as we can, we will be met with understanding and forgiveness. Universal justice always prevails. "The lip of truth shall be established for ever: but a lying tongue is but for a moment"*(Proverbs 12:19)*.

There is no doubt that deception is rampant "in high places" in our society. This is reflected in our wavering trust in politicians, major institutions, and professionals. Any person who intentionally deceives large groups of people or misleads someone who holds an office of power carries an enormous burden in his soul. He can cause irreparable harm to society and to the world by limiting or biasing people's choices. History attests to the fact that influential leaders who manipulated the minds of their countrymen started wars with grave consequences. During the earthly life and beyond, their souls will remain burdened by their horrific act of genocide as the crying of the brutally murdered resonates throughout the Universe. A truthful alternative would have been better for everyone, even if the immediate outcome was unpleasant. Gandhi's philosophy of "satyagraha" is based on the concept that truth must be the foundation of any moral action, and that continuous commitment to the truth is the only reason for our existence. Based on his faith in the inherent presence of absolute truth in each human being, Gandhi used the moral power of this concept to unite Hindus and Muslims under the social cause of nonviolent resistance toward others, thus galvanizing India to stand tall against British rule.

The Universe rewards truth in the long run. The words of Jesus, "ye shall know the truth, and the truth shall make you free," *(John 8:32)* must never be forgotten. These wise words do not refer to the earthly freedom of action in the materialistic world. They imply supreme freedom from the bondage of constraining personal beliefs, which can be granted only to those who strive to approach the absolute truth. Although these words resonate in all modern world religions, more and more people get tangled in the web of lying to create an illusion of temporary satisfaction. They fail to understand that they are sinking deeper into the sea of disharmony, deceit, and regret. Adopting lying and deception as a way of life, they continue to damage their integrity and lose their sense of self-worth, which is characteristic only to the human race. Unfortunately, lying is gaining ground at all levels of society.

Physicians are our earthly healers. They are to be respected for their knowledge and talent. Doctors often have the unenviable task of telling a patient that he is terminally ill. A good doctor is not only skilled in the mechanics of the body, but also in the art of being human. He cannot lie. To do this is to dishonor the patient and himself. A doctor understands that by withholding the truth he limits his patient's choices. Perhaps when a patient knows his stay on this planet is coming to an end, he would choose not to submit to unnecessary and painful treatments. Also, deceiving a patient does not give him time to put his affairs in order, to seek closure with people and experiences in his life, and the right to decide where he will end his earthly pilgrimage. A physician has a difficult job. He must tell the truth about a terminal diagnosis without robbing a person of hope. After all, miracles occur everyday.

Today, the meaning of politics has extended its use from the service of government to organizations that employ thousands of people. This new "professional quality" is becoming common throughout the work place. Politics is accepted across the entire spectrum of economic activity, which encompasses international relations, government, businesses, educational institutions, and various nonprofit organizations. Most managers and politicians possess diplomatic abilities and lead in accordance with truthful principles. In so doing, they can safeguard the company's profitability and guarantee the satisfaction of their supporters. The art of dealing with people at an ethical and constructive level stems from the ability to reason. Sometimes, within business settings, unreasonable, overconfident, and inept low-level managers manipulate the power of their positions to materialize their demonic dreams of increasing their authority over others, to influence events, and to exploit every opportunity for their personal gain. Their Machiavellian mind-set does not allow them to see failure as an opportunity for improvement, thus lying and finger pointing becomes their instantaneous salvation. The hypocrisy of unethical politics was well described by Ronald Reagan as being the "the second oldest profession," which "bears a very close resemblance to the first." Generally, those who misunderstand their position of elusive temporary power over others are misguided human beings who consciously try to project a false appearance of satisfaction. These are arrogant people who confuse self-worth with social status, thus missing the focal point of social intercourse: all human beings deserve respect for who they are, and not for what they do. In order to perpetuate the false image of their indispensable contribution to the work place and to society in general, which usually manifests in the destruction of assets and the victimizing of people, they deceive themselves with visions of magnanimity to the point of displaying the emptiness of their souls through their body language. Speaking condescendingly to colleagues, and continuously wearing a false smile are only some of the common symptoms of physical deceit. These are the people who are either unable to admit, or refuse to accept that the "highway" from their psychological misery to the ever distancing road to happiness is passing under the tunnel of truth, so they continue to avoid this road and keep on wallowing in self-deceit.

Self-deception represents the pinnacle of deceit. It is a superficial rationalization chosen by people to mask the truth. The self-deceiver has developed the habit to disguise the truth in such a way that he creates for himself an impression of sincerity. Initially, the self-deceiver chooses careful manipulations of language as a veil for concealing the truth. In time, deception becomes his reality. The irrationality of self-deception is that after making it a daily habit, many people develop the perfect mental system to choose deception as their "true reality," and then to be satisfied with this mindset. With continuous reinforcement, some can even pass a lie detector test. All human beings have the capacity for self-deceit. Concealing one's age is a very common self-deception. Nevertheless, this is the basic mechanism of promotion for the cosmetics industry. Although looking younger is definitely a preference in the Western society, it is self-deceptive to confuse the reality of young looks, which can boost one's ego for a moment, with the truth of the countable age. From going to movies to watching sports, we run continuously from our daily reality to other man made realities. As long as we understand our role as spectators and not as participants in these chosen escapes from the truth, the mental paradox of self-deception will be avoided and many hours of relaxation can be enjoyed. Self-deception can have positive effects, or it can lead to crimes and other evil actions. One can never forget that self-deception is a creation of the mind, which usually besmirches the pure truth of the soul and squeezes the happiness out of life. Building a mindset of sincerity is the only protection against the plague of self-deception.

It is common for people to find excusable the deceit of their own children. Parents feel the need to protect their children from bad news. Once again, the kindest truth is the preferred path. Children, like adults, should know about situations that will affect their lives. They have the right to know about adoption and divorce. If a parent or anyone close to the child is misleading or deceptive about an issue and is then caught, that child's soul is irreparably shattered. Also, one deception leads to others. This "living a lie" can be exhausting and psychologically debilitating by damaging our sense of human self-worth. Tell the truth and you don't need excuses and explanations. It is difficult sometimes not to lie because one feels power in his ability to manipulate a child under the disguise of paternalism. Lying feeds the ego. From deceiving a child "for his own good," to sending an innocent party to prison for the good of the liar, one must realize that he is disgracing his soul and is misusing the articulate language, which was entrusted to man to serve humanity, not to destroy it. However, one rarely takes into consideration the consequences of lies, or how it feels to the deceived to have their trust shattered forever. Deceit can take a life long toll on our relationships with our children.

The mind, the presenter of our own reality, separates us from the truth. Always adhering to the earthly truth, which is the verbal projection of the soul, will help us to gradually advance on the endless journey towards the absolute truth. The willingness to train one's mind to always use truthful diplomacy in all issues of life is a basic prerequisite for social interaction. Only truth will bond mankind. Only truth will encourage intimacy instead of paranoia and mistrust. Only honesty and trust will guarantee peace. According to Indian wisdom, "when your mind and your heart are pure, then the divine will be open." This is a good piece of advice from people who were lied to and deceived. Improving this world, and all the worlds to come by reinstating the everlasting ethical value of honesty and sincerity is the only road to eternal truth. Being truthful is a magnificent way to travel on the last stretch to God.

4

Faith

"All the scholastic scaffolding falls, as a ruined edifice, before one single word-faith."

—*Napoleon Bonaparte*

F aith is an unbiased system of complete confidence and unquestioning trust without any logical proof or factual evidence. It is an absolute certainty so ingrained within man's soul that he wouldn't even think to question it. Faith excludes intellectual pondering. Being an unequivocal trust, when you have faith, you know that you know. Faith is a combination of instinct, a remainder from the subhuman origin and desire, and a characteristic of human evolution. The ability to rely on faith differs immensely from individual to individual. By itself, knowledge is an enemy of faith. However, when these two human characteristics are able to join in one's personality, great achievements usually follow.

The most triumphant people in human history have been knowledgeable individuals with a great deal of faith. From Moses to Martin Luther King, and from Marco Polo to John Glenn, courage, knowledge, and faith helped them make an incredible contribution to humanity. Under cautious scrutiny, one can find that even the axioms of reason are based on faith. From the most materialistic human being, who does not realize that every day of his life is a miracle, to the most idealistic person, who sees God in everything, faith is a necessary ingredient of human existence.

Pragmatically, a miracle is a phenomenon, which contradicts scientific thought. Repeated similar miracles become fertile ground for science. For the primitive man, the night following the day, the sun shining, the moon glowing at night, and the flowers germinating from seeds were all miracles. Today, the explanation of these phenomena is covered in the first course of elementary science for children all over the world. Although one can have faith in various principles and ideals, all of us, without even realizing it, have faith to some degree in the comprehensive logic and the perfect order of the Universe. Science tries to elucidate the miracle of life, while religion interprets miracles as theistic proofs of the *perfection of the Universe*, the omnipotent God. Since the beginning of human civilization, various myths conveyed the idea that the Universe responded to man's faith according to a preconceived agreement between himself and various deities. Although some religions believe in an anthropomorphic God, today's scientist usually sees him as a perfect creator whose presence is symbolized by the absolute truth.

Why would we need faith when we have science? While one of them may be enough for most people, the human race needs both. Absolute certainty of knowledge is by no means a guarantee of security in life. The ideal evidence can only be attained in mathematics, where concepts like infinity and zero have a meaning, which is given by the highest level of abstraction characteristic to the "language of nature." As soon as these concepts have to be applied in physics, chemistry, and biology we are lost, and we immediately run for cover with words like "unrealizable" or "unachievable." The concrete nature of theoretical sciences, which are "mirrors of nature," requires faith. Scientists are probably the biggest connoisseurs of faith. The seventeenth century's British physicist, Robert Boyle, a pioneer in the study of thermodynamics of gases, was also a devout Christian. After his death, the Boyle lectures were established for the sole purpose of Christian education.

Boyle's contemporary, the French physicist, mathematician, and philosopher René Descartes had been a great believer in the perfection of the Universe. In the twentieth century, the American physicist Albert Einstein, by combining his knowledge in physics with his unwavering faith in the order of the Universe, developed the revolutionary Theory of Relativity. The list of representatives of genius in many fields of science, humanities, and arts will never end. They all had, and will continue to have faith in the truth, in the goodness of nature, in their fellow man, and in the exquisite elegance of the perfect Universe. In their search for new bits of knowledge, they follow the old Latin adage, "Believe, that you may understand."

If "exact sciences" cannot offer us an absolute description of reality, can philosophy decipher the mysteries of human life? Because of the continuous evolution of the human brain, we have started to question our position in time, space, and society. The animal kingdom has solved this problem of uncertainty by always living in the present within his surrounding space. When the immediate needs of an animal are satisfied, certainty of the future is not a consideration. Tomorrow is not promised to anyone. It is human intelligence that invented the future, and thus we need guarantees. Although the future is only an expectation, human beings use faith as a temporary support, while waiting for the future to become the present and finally vanish into the past. This is the temporal aspect of faith. Can we ever know if we understand other people, or even be sure that we always understand ourselves? Can we always know that doing the best that we can, will bring us the projected outcome? It is this philosophical aspect of faith that keeps us traveling from birth to death while surviving within our society. If man would know his destiny in advance, then the secrecy of human life, which is filled with doubt, anxiety, and hope could not exist. The happy surprises of life are the result of intelligent and timely decisions based on knowledge coupled with infinite faith. Children have faith in Santa, and parents make sure that his visit on Christmas is always a happy surprise. The opposite is true for the big disappointments of life. Adults cannot rely on parents to be the substitutes for Santa. Many times they have to make choices, which go beyond reason. Depending on the individual's upbringing, his life experience, and his understanding of the world, he makes decisions based on knowledge, faith in himself and other people, and in the absolute perfection of the Universe, which religions around the world view as God. Throughout time, man has tried to understand and describe the perfection of the Universe. But how can he measure the infinite perfection of ultimate reality with instruments of finite accuracy, or explain it with the limited capabilities of various imperfect languages? Indian wisdom defines faith in most descriptive words: "Those who have only the knowledge which can be received by our five senses do not know the essence of things. Real knowledge is the understanding that is an inner being in everything."

As man's instinctive adaptation diminished, which is characteristic to the animal, he entered a new world of an indefinite and doubtful type of existence bound by two definite temporal events: the known birth date, and the unknown death moment. Having no control over the length and quality of his stay on the Earth, if man tries to use only his will to navigate through life, then he usually finds himself a prisoner to his own loneliness when his parents, children, siblings, and friends unexpectedly leave him. The huge forces of nature and society render him helpless and alone, so that he has inevitably to run to faith in order to complete his existence. The price paid for the power to reason, which is characteristic only to the human race, led to his irretrievable loss of instinctual harmony, which is characteristic to the animal kingdom. The awareness of his relatively short human life span, as man considers himself separate from the oneness of the Universe, is his biggest source of uncertainty and anxiety. As life presents opportunities to feed their egos, it is this void of insecurity, which some people mistakenly try to fill by securing power over others. Usually, these are dangerous people with limited ability to value nature and society, and who try to hide behind false religious beliefs or illusions of knowledge. As they search to find any sense of unity in their lonely world, they try to achieve temporary satisfaction through power games based on the relinquishing of personal reason, and putting all their faith in their superior's orders. In time, due to their insecurities, they attempt other illogical escapes as their superiority complex blinds them. As wholeness becomes more and more elusive, and when the wisdom acquired through life starts to show its use, they may allow faith to become their safety net. In this case they finally join the people, who understand that it is faith in the perfect Universe that transfigures man's life from a prison of doubt to a liberated eternal future. Although man's faith in others, or even in himself can be shattered throughout life, his faith in the eternal order and perfection of the Universe will always remain a timeless support.

The concept of faith is as old as the human race. The faith in gods can be found in all ancient civilizations. Hinduism describes the miracles of some of their deities in the Puranas (ancient stories). The deity of Vishnu solves many difficult life situations by materializing into anthropomorphic beings like his avatar Krishna, or into animal forms living on the Earth or in the water. Buddha's conception and his sanctified descent into the human world through his mother's womb, and his human birth is a miracle. As a human being, Buddha considered himself a teacher of divine knowledge and not a miracle worker.

The world's major monotheistic religions are all a declaration of faith in one God. According to the Old Testament, Abraham "believed in the Lord: and he counted it to him for righteousness" *(Genesis 15:6)*. In the rabbinic literature, the word *emunah* (faith) is generally translated as trust in the righteousness of God. A famous rabbi once said that one who still has bread in his basket and ponders on what shall he eat tomorrow "belongs to those who are small in faith." Jesus explained to his disciples that faith is the foundation of miracles: "If ye have faith as a grain of mustard seed, ye shall say unto this mountain. Remove hence to yonder place; and it shall remove; and nothing shall be impossible to you" *(Matthew 17:20)*. Probably one of the best definitions of faith is found in the New Testament. "Faith is the substance of things hoped for, the evidence of things not seen" *(Hebrews 11:1)*.

The Old Testament story of Rahab's faith in God, which guided her to save the lives of the Israelites from the king of Jericho is unforgettable. Consequently, Joshua's army "saved the harlot alive, and her father's household" *(Joshua 6:25)*. In spite of being called a harlot, she proved to be a woman of faith. Along with other examples of faith, the New Testament references Rahab's action as a display of trust in God. It was "by faith the harlot Rahab perished not with them that believed not, when she had received the spies with peace" *(Hebrews 11:31)*.

All modern religions are founded on faith. Muslims must declare their faith in God seventeen times a day. The first pillar of Islam, *Shahadah*, which translates into "witnessing," is the Muslims' declaration of faith in the existence of one God and in his prophet Muhammad. The "Bearing Witness" pillar represents the testimony of *iman* (faith) of the believers. According to the Bhagavad Gita, the holy scripture of Hinduism, "man is made by his belief. As he believes, so he is." Chinese people say that "only a man who has faith is good," and having faith "is when your will is in consent with the world's conscience and the world's wisdom" (Tao). According to the Buddhist wisdom of Dhammapada, if a man's faith is not firmly internalized, he can never acquire perfect knowledge.

The sacred scriptures of various groups of people are rich in miracles, which illustrate the grandiose drama of creation, development, and final extinction of the human race as a self revelation of the omnipotent power which is the origin of all: God. In the Old Testament one can find many instances when God's unlimited love protects man throughout his daily existence. The incredible crossing of the Red Sea by the liberated Israelite slaves, thus saving the people of Israel and swallowing the Pharaoh's chariots, is the greatest miracle of the Old Testament. Because the Jewish faith views life as a continuous marvel (mofet) of God, "the person to whom a miracle happens is not aware of it himself." *(Talmud)* The miracles of Jesus can be found throughout the New Testament. The healing of a leper, a woman with internal bleeding, a blind man, a noble man's son and his own resurrection are only a few examples of miracles performed by the Son of Man. The faithful Muslims believe that every chapter of the Qur'an represents a miracle of God (i'jaz). Other Islamic literature lists many miracles performed by Muhammad. In the Qur'an, the Prophet describes himself as a plain messenger, while Allah has the miracle making power. No one can deny the extraordinary order of our Universe, its exquisite and perfect design, the symbiotic relationships between organisms, and the complexities of the biological world when we continuously witness the miracle of perfection unfolding before our eyes.

Faith has stood the test of time. While nations have eliminated slavery, monarchies, feudalism, and communism faith continues to flourish in our modern age. Many people choose to believe that the purpose and meaning of human existence can only be a stratagem of a higher power, while others are still looking for final theories. Whether one is a proponent of the Big Bang Theory of creation, the Strings Theory, or the evolution of the human species, he will reluctantly admit that these theories are far from perfect in explaining our existence. Although quantum physics provides an elegant explanation of many things, it does not cover everything. A quantum leap of faith is needed to explain the Principle of Indeterminism. Faced with the ideas that "continuous motion" must be substituted with "disjointed jumps" between unpredictable places, and that the observer and the observed properties of matter are dependent on each other, man is still forced to rely on miracles, as physics and consciousness begin to overlap. It is much easier to look at the Universe as being a sequence of consecutive scenes in the grand opera of life, as being directed by an unknown Supreme Power, who chooses to keep the spectators in suspense until the final fall of the curtain. We, the earthly spectators, will continue to labor to understand the thinking of this Unknown Director. As new details are revealed to questioning minds, some begin to realize that "miracles happen only to those who believe in them," as a wise French proverb says. These are the ones who enjoy the show, and in their minds, choose to become a part of it. Unfortunately, others are asking to be reimbursed for their tickets, although they remain mesmerized by the first scene. These are the majority, who completely missed the opportunity to comprehend the miracle of life, as their imagination struggles to overcome their thirst for immediate reality. This is not the case for anyone who has had a mystical experience, an instantaneous healing, or other close encounters with the divine perfection of the Universe, and thus discovered the meaning of a miracle outside of the Opera House. Although such experiences are solely personal in nature, and cannot be understood and quantified by the human mind, one cannot so easily dismiss them as hallucinations or aberrations in brain physiology, without making a mockery of the experience.

Armed with faith, man alone can defend himself against uncertainty, fear, and doubt. In times of adversity, one begins to internalize the perfection of the Universe to support nature, and consequently chooses to be a part of it. His faith strengthens and it becomes extremely real. This is a time of boundless ebullience. Clear direction, peace, self-satisfaction, and happiness are the inevitable outcomes of the integration of faith into the psychic makeup of the human being. Although gifted only to humans, faith is not always practiced. Thus man changes his everlasting joyful life, and is condemned to survive in the misery of his attachment to the material world. This is his choice of a grim reality of complete evanescence, as the body is either cremated or lowered into the grave at death time.

Faith and patience are needed during difficult times. One needs to remain steadfast in one's beliefs and never stop visualizing the desired outcome. The Universe reacts to faith in ways that are not always known to man. One's life is continually adjusted as reason and faith work in concert to align his destiny with the Universal plan for mankind. Remaining faithful during the winding journey of life is of unquestionable importance. This is a unique period when the Universe molds and develops man's character, thus preparing him for something better. One day during life's journey, the fog will lift to reveal a bright sunny day. At that time, it becomes crystal clear that the Universe had been man's shadow all along. It becomes obvious that faith is not a tranquilizer or a sedative taken to mask the tragedies and wretchedness of modern day life. It is not for the weak or the escapist, but for the brave at heart. Faith is for the one who wants to confront the harshness of life with all its pain and struggles. Faith is for the one with a strong psyche and a questioning mind. It is for the one who is not content with simple answers. Faith is for the relentless seeker of the truth.

The secret is to consciously understand, and subconsciously internalize that the events of one man's life influences all mankind. Human beings empowered with reason, knowledge, and faith must lead all living creatures in a common effort to align with the Universal order, which masterminds the life of our planet for the good of all. Together we are the co-creators of this drama. Today the world is in an endless state of turmoil. Wrongdoers throughout the world are misguided lost souls at all levels of society. Rogue governments and irrational individuals, driven by satanic dreams to control the world through violence and war, distort the faith of the young and of the old, thus promoting and practicing terror to achieve the impossible: to correct the already perfect Universe. They refuse to understand that trying to adjust divine perfection to suit their deranged design will only lead to the destruction of our planet. After looking everywhere, and finding nothing to have faith in, human beings either accept freely or accept to be convinced to become loyal to causes and principles. Some of these oppose the human value of the sanctity of life, thus defying reason, reneging on the promise of science, and disregarding the true teaching of all religions: human life comes first in the eyes of the Universe. They become perpetuators of terror, who accept to sacrifice their lives for the evil purpose of obliterating as much life as possible in the name of faith. This is the danger of misusing faith. It is apparent that faith, one of the most powerful components of the human race, can be used as one of the riskiest weapons against mankind. Any war led by an irrational belief in ferocious acts can cause thousands of victims, if terror spreads throughout the world. If the promoters of such wars refuse to recognize the danger of distorting faith, then humanity will be their last casualty.

There is another way. Men of all races, colors, and religions must have faith, and find their own purpose for existence, thus tuning their lives to the Universal rhythm. Each and every one of us was put on this Earth for a reason. We are all on a united mission to serve, learn, and evolve toward full enlightenment. As the number of people increases exponentially, and the natural resources are not able to supply the ever-growing need, faith in the bright future of man on this planet must be encouraged by responsible scientists, teachers, clergymen, and parents. We are here to learn, to enlighten, and to transfer our knowledge to others who are in need, and to make their lives more comfortable. Through knowledge, mankind has made progress by making the world smaller and we can hear from each other via communication channels, which were unimaginable half a century ago. Although we are scattered around the globe, with the advent of the World-Wide-Web, we can influence each other from the comfort of our living rooms. Faith in the wisdom of the Universe is needed more now than ever. Many times prayers seem to go unanswered. Sometimes, the answers can be different than what one may want or think he needs. Our only guarantee is that the laws of the Universe are working perfectly. Through science, faith, and meditation, man can take advantage of them, even though not all of them are known.

The American Indian will forever remain a great example of living with faith. He appreciated his spiritual blessings. He instinctively communed with the Universe. He worshipped alone and in silence. There were no churches, temples, or shrines. The Indian felt no need for such things as he preferred to worship in God's real cathedral under the canopy of stars, surrounded by all of God's creations in the carpeted green forests, the vast prairies, and majestic mountains. The Indian never sought to convert anyone to his way of thinking. There were no priests or sermons. No one was allowed to influence his faith, or to interfere with the religious experience of another. Being unknowledgeable of cause and effect, the Indian had faith in an unseen force. To him, it was all a miracle. He witnessed miracles every day in the birth of all earthly creatures, the warmth of the sun, the spring harvest, and the magnificent forces of nature. The Indian had faith that the Universe would provide him with all of his needs. He knew there would be plenty of animals for him to hunt, providing him with food, clothing, and weapons. He revered these animals, as the Indian believed that all living creatures to some degree have a soul, and therefore he was grateful that they would offer themselves up to aid his survival. The Indians loved and respected his friends of the animal kingdom, considered them pure, and was humbled by what they perceived to be a voluntary sacrifice of their life to preserve his own.

The Native American felt no need to emulate the accomplishments of the white man. He felt no need for fame or competition. He felt no need for self-glorification. To him all men were sons of the creator and were to be treated with respect. It was an honor and a responsibility to share with his less fortunate brothers. His spirit was free from greed, envy, and lust. The Indian felt that his creator expected him to live a simple life. His belief prohibited the accumulation of wealth and luxurious living. It would be a sacrilege to denounce all that was given to him by the Universe and presume to build a more desirable complex society filled with needless temptations. He knew that the Universe set no value on material things, and therefore when he worshipped he took with him only simple sacrifices. He wore the simplest clothes and slept under the awning of the stars. "The greatest virtue is not to do evil, even to our enemies," represents one of the strong beliefs of Indian Wisdom.

It is a human conundrum that people have faith in computers, airplanes, cars, and other man-made devices without having the slightest knowledge of how these inventions function. They trust not only their finances and major life decisions to this equipment, but often their physical lives. Meditation and visualization are the only direct personal communication between the human mind and the perfect Universe. So many miracles, both large and small have been accomplished through visualization and prayer. Only a quiet, attentive mind can detect signals through the stillness of infinity. Many answers to various questions are offered when man lowers the noise level created by daily living, and listens to the penetrating signals. One needs to be patient and have faith. The virtue of patience is required to allow the inner feelings generated by faith to confront challenges and produce winning strategies for smooth sailing through the earthly life. If we doubt, some answers may come to us not from the Universe, but from experiences on the earthly plane, which we would rather not have. When we have faith in our oneness with the Universe, perfect answers will come to us in unexpected ways. Sometimes answers come during meditative states or during quiet moments in the form of a thought or an inspiration. Sometimes they appear through an intuition. Listen to them and act accordingly. Many answers may approach us through synchronicity, which is a non-local interface between all components of the eternal Universe. How many times did we find ourselves in the right place at the right time? How many times did we unexpectedly meet someone who could help us, or found that object that we considered lost? Synchronicity is purposeful! This is how the perfection of the Universe is displayed to the trained observer. For most, it appears to be a lucky break and not a call back to them. "Let us have faith that right makes might, and in that faith let us to the end dare to do our duty as we understand it," said Abraham Lincoln at an address at the Copper Union almost a century and a half ago.

The Peace Pilgrim made it her duty to show the world what faith is all about. Better known as a "wandering nun," she had unwavering faith in the Universe. She began her spiritual journey in India begging for food and shelter, sharing her spiritual thoughts, and accepting what the Universe chose to provide for her. Between the ages of forty-four and seventy-three, she traveled the entire United States, the ten provinces of Canada, and parts of Mexico entirely by foot without money, food, medicine, or a change of clothes. Peace Pilgrim had unwavering faith in herself, in other human beings, and in the Universe that she would be provided with all that she needed to make this grandiose journey. She preached love, detachment from material things, and the living of a simpler, less burdensome life. She had incredible courage, perseverance, and uncompromising faith. She was a true spiritual athlete. Her faith is what gave her and continuously gives man the inspiration, courage, and determination to achieve, regardless of the obstacles thrown in their way. Faith is behind all human achievement, and can make the difference between success and failure. By aligning our lives with the perfect laws of the Universe, we will be able to leave a legacy that will enrich others, as we transcend the unseen border between our earthly existence and the eternal Universe. Only in this way will the world continue to be what it was designed to be: a peaceful, loving, and blissful home for all.

Many human actions are far from perfect or sometimes even mean spirited. As faithful members of society, we all have the duty to stop them. No one may forget that mankind developed as an image of perfection, which implies taking actions based on faith in a personal bright future within the permanency of the Universe. What one receives during his earthly stay is the result of the inner workings of the Universal order. Every decision or action carried out by other animated beings, and all natural phenomena involving unconscious matter make a contribution in supporting faith. Perhaps we will need to go through difficult times, during which we were meant to learn valuable lessons, to gain wisdom, and to become stronger. However, hope is not enough. While faith, as defined by organized religion, is an individual's choice, faith in the perfection of the Universe and in the goodness of our fellow man is a requirement for the further survival of humankind. With effort and faith one will never be defeated. Having faith in the perfection of the Universe is a magnificent way to travel on the last stretch to God.

5

The Environment

"Nature to be commanded must be obeyed."

—*Francis Bacon*

At the turn of this millennium, the Earth was approximately five billion years old and human civilization celebrated its six-thousandth birthday. As modern tribes were lighting the sky with fire around the globe, the biosphere was being sabotaged by the organized scraping of the bottom of oceans, by the hunting of jungle animals, and by the cutting of trees in the rainforests in the name of progress.

Almost four decades ago, referring to global instability, John F. Kennedy told the world that "the vulnerability of our planet" is a "supreme reality" *(Speech on June 28, 1963).* Although a nuclear war may be avoided, the world is set upon another course of destabilizing our planet through the relentless destruction of the environment, which maintains it. Already proven by numerous photographs taken by satellites or by astronauts, it is clear that mankind's survival depends on one limited resource that we call "Earth." In order to expect continuous life support in the future, the Earth and natural environment must be carefully maintained. Ravaging nature, polluting the environment, destroying the plant and animal kingdoms, and wasting natural resources are actions guaranteed to bring us very close to global biological collapse.

The present complacency of people will not be in any way rewarded at the end of history. At that time, the rich and the pure alike, will have no place to hide from the consequences of the present irresponsible destruction of the planet. It is too late to completely undo the past, but individuals and governments must be now more aware than ever, that the past and the present determine the unique geological and ecological future, which does not look very bright from the vantage point of today.

The difficulty to understand this irreparable condition perpetuated by man stems from the lack of responsibility of the masses, the lack of coverage by the media, and by disinterested governments, which are busy reacting to the immediate economic and political pressures of the present world. As history never repeats itself in the exact same way, and those who were not capable to observe the subtle changes developed in time were left behind, the inconsiderate doctrine that "each generation will find a method of survival" will not work again. Because the planet's life as we know it is maintained by an ecologic and atmospheric control system in which the lack of restraint has been compensated for by international laws designed to curtail excessive damage, the system has worked for thousand of years. This subtle change, which began at the middle of the last century, took place in an environment of population explosion. This is pervasive in under-developed countries, where the polarization of wealth is being encouraged through distorted religious fundamentalism. At the same time, a new culture of excessive consumption, and irresponsible indolence, nourished by the excessive availability of material goods, has been created in developed countries. There are many concerned individuals whose voices of desperation are not being heard. These are people who realize the effects of the present lethargy of the international community to correct the human disaster, which is unraveling in front of their eyes. Although they shout for help to preserve their lives, their children's lives, and their grandchildren's existence, their voices are being muffled by the immediate needs of governments to abate localized wars and protect innocent citizens from the new wave of international terrorism.

Malthusian theory of disharmony between population growth and food supply, proposed by the British economist Robert Malthus at the end of the eighteenth century, states that while the population increase takes place at a geometric rate, the food supply grows at an arithmetical rate. It will prove to be correct at the beginning of the third millennium. Of course, Malthus's thesis was not embraced by most economists because of its unacceptable consequences, that of famine, disease, early mortality, and wars for existence. Today, tens of thousands of people, mainly children, die of malnutrition every day. His thesis proved to be valid in the animal kingdom, as species unsupported by nature have become extinct through predation. The capacity for destruction of various species by man alone has been greatly increased by advances in technology, so that the seemingly uncontrolled elimination of plant and animal life on land, on the bottom of lakes, rivers, and oceans are considered industries.

All wars have economic roots, although they have been well obscured by social causes. They are driven by the incessant desire to have more, or by the need of those who have nothing to get their fair share. This process will continue until the end of the Earth. After all, it does seem that Malthus was neither pessimistic nor incorrect. Unfortunately, he was a visionary social thinker whose theory cannot be accepted due to its sad, but true prophetic character. Does this mean that man cannot slow down the recent acceleration toward the Messianic revelation? Does this mean that we have to rush to waste our world's resources so that nothing will be left for the coming generations? Does this mean that holocausts have to be tolerated for the benefit of their perpetrators? "*No*" is the resounding answer to these frightening possibilities. Before beginning to work towards a solution, man must use his unique capacity to reason, and become fully aware of the possible consequences through education. It is sufficient to look at today's status reached by mankind within the context of life on Earth.

As any change of course in history is painful, measures must be taken to assure its final success. The education of all people must become the highest priority of all governments around the world. The irresponsible waste of food by those who can afford it must be stopped, as they will have to realize that "it is not just money." The promotion of terror used by those with grand plans of world supremacy must be stopped, either diplomatically or by military defeat, as they refuse to understand that a return to feudalism and tyrannical oppression of the masses is not viable today. Freedom guaranteed by democratic governments and cooperation among people is the only key by which to preserve the future of mankind. One can never overlook that we are not created equal and Utopia cannot be achieved.

Literature and the World Wide Web contain numerous examples, which show modern man's total disregard for life and his environment. It is a common practice for millions of commercial fishing boats to use trawling, long lining, and dynamite coral reef fishing. In the waters surrounding the United States, various species of fish such as Pacific salmon, red snapper, swordfish, and some sharks are being decimated, while other water creatures are being born deformed. The website of Earth Crash Earth Spirit *(http://eces.org)* reports daily many crimes against the environment. Whales are being killed by collisions with boats and the Yellow River of China is becoming a deposit of toxic materials. Africa's Lake Victoria is being polluted by sewage and recreational boats on the coast of India are destroying the endangered species of the Irrawaddy Dolphins. The wild Atlantic Salmon are disappearing in the water of the River Nore in Ireland. On the Earth, species of plants are becoming extinct, due to the increasing use of pesticides, and the irrational collecting of flowers for garden shops. Black Rhinos and the Paddington Bear are on the brink of extinction. The illegal commerce of ivory, wild animal products, and unusual birds threaten the ecosystem of the Earth. These are only a few examples of irresponsible ecological crimes.

The planet is being stressed to its maximum. The ozone layer protecting the Earth from excessive damaging ultraviolet radiation is being depleted, while the pollution of rivers and lakes reduces the supply of fish for many communities. At the same time, oceans are being emptied of marine life with the most sophisticated technology. Every attack on humans by hungry sharks coming close to the shore to look for food makes national news. It is not their beastly instinct to harm; it is man's ignorance, which leaves them hungry. The agricultural soil is being excessively utilized to produce food for an increasing number of people, which can be measured in billions per decade while the forests and animal species are being destroyed at an accelerated pace, all in the name of progress and development.

According to our own assessment, humans are the most intelligent inhabitants on the planet. When this conclusion is drawn, some important facts must be included in the overall view. Only in the present century, at least eight billion people will live on the Earth. Each one will require millions of cubic feet of oxygen and tons of food during his lifetime. The polluting of the environment and the depleting of natural resources must be stopped. The greenhouse effect, intensified through air pollution, which increases the carbon dioxide concentration in the air, and increases the temperature of the atmosphere, must be controlled. As a result of these changes, the appearance of new unfriendly bacteria that can attack us will be exacerbated. Man cannot afford to continue to disturb the balance of the ecosystem with modern machinery. Each extinct creature is another missing link in the food chain. Did we become the smartest or the meanest animals in the kingdom?

The continuous deforestation of land in order to make unnecessary amounts of paper, furniture, and home decor displaces and destroys billions of creatures, both large and small. Being unable to adapt to living in a foreign place, these displaced animals die. In the forests, people are brutally killing millions of animals. They are systematically murdering defenseless beings for fur coats, boots, jewelry, and purses. This is murder of the worst kind. Man is taking advantage of beings with less ability to reason and communicate. Humans are killing their brothers and sisters, as we are all creatures of this Universe. Irrational eradication of animal life in the water and on the ground is harming us in many known and some unknown ways.

Scraping the bottoms of oceans is a multi-billion dollar industry. The uncontrolled dumping of chemicals and toxic waste into waters, disregarding that these places house millions of creatures, is now called, "doing business." As a result, marine life will cease to exist. How quickly we have forgotten our roots! We modeled our life after the grandiose design of the Universe. Family life appeared for the need of support between its members. Does the fact that the fish is a creature of lesser intelligence make it less valuable to the Universe? The answer is without a doubt, *"no."* The perfection of the Universe requires everything that was ever created, so that the symphony of life will harmonize the lives of all creatures.

The rain forests are disappearing. The animals that inhabit them are becoming extinct, and as trees are being cut down, so is living creatures' supply of oxygen. This organized and indiscriminant cutting of trees and plants drastically reduces the oxygen production through photosynthesis. We are really destroying the hand that feeds us. Humans are feeding the Earth chemicals to make crops grow larger, and to force the soil to produce at an unnatural rate. Did the primitive man do this? No, he did not, as he was satisfied to take only what he *needed* to live. How can anyone not realize that while children are starving all over the world, we let food rot in our refrigerators? Unfortunately, it is a reality of our modern time to value life in dollars; thus it is only normal to equate waste of life resources with loss of money.

The Universal design of nature is characterized by a profound logic that we can only partially understand. According to the Darwinian Theory of Evolution, the food chain guarantees the continuity of life. Each species has a role in the evolutionary process, which must be played in order to assure the success of the drama of life. It evolves to fill a void, and it becomes extinct when excess is created. In this zero-sum game of life, when one species gains by a large advantage at the expense of their opponent's extinction, the marvelous architecture of nature is placed at risk. Modern man's satisfaction to hoard and waste resources of life, and the mass murdering of animal life, was never intended in the blueprint of evolution. Living with the illusion of becoming the strongest player in his mindless game against nature, man has forgotten the dynamics of his physical existence, thus trying to justify his irrational pillage of nature in the name of "civilization" and "progress." The implication of a zero-sum game is that the winning player maximizes the opponent's losses by maximizing the effects of the accepted rules of the game. The use of high technology is not one of the rules. The developed power to reason based on the incorrect assumption that the other species are his "opponents," leads man on his blind quest of being the final loser. Although animals do not have the symbolic intelligence similar to that of humans who are aware of the relative direction of time, they are endowed with various degrees of intelligence. Always living in the present, they sense pleasure and fear in the same way man does. They are not man's opponents. On the contrary, they coexist for the perfect functioning of Earth's planetary order. Killing an animal for any reason other than the need for food is similar to unnecessarily committing a crime and pointlessly disturbing the rules of oneness of life. The Universe, in its perfect order, is the only one that can give and take life. It has done this with perfection through the food chain and natural selection. Universal order determines when a plant's, an animal's, or a human's purpose in the game of life has been fulfilled. At our current state of social development hunting is considered a game, and according to human justice no crime has been committed. It is time to understand that disturbing the natural order set by the Universe for temporary enjoyment is wrong.

For Kabbalists, Wisdom and Understanding constitute an imaginary bridge between the inexpressible God (the Crown) from above, and the rest of the worlds located at the lower levels of the Tree of Life.

For them, wisdom is a reflection of the oneness of the Universe, the eternal connectedness with all Creation. Kabbalah teaches its practitioners neither to harm, nor to kill plants and animals unless it is absolutely needed for man's sustenance. Thus, it becomes apparent that our food comes from the Universe, which maintains us as an integrated component of planetary existence. Thanking God for the food provided to us before each meal can be viewed as a reinforcement of the awareness of man's unity with the plants and animals created by God. Kabbalists understand that while man has a different role than animals in the drama of Creation, he is not the owner of the script. Therefore, abusing his unique power to reason, by harming the rest of Creation will certainly lead to the final destruction of the Earth. It seemed like déjà vu when Albert Einstein, the most famous physicist of all times, echoed this Kabbalistic teaching from the medieval era in the twentieth century, when he advised us to "require a substantially new manner of thinking if mankind is to survive," as he reflected on man's delusion with his assumed power.

Due to his arrogance and conviction to win a losing game, man has stopped listening to reason. Without having any hard evidence of being at fault, it seems that man is being punished with mudslides, fires, avalanches, tornadoes, and earthquakes in the natural environment, and with wars and terror in the social environment. These are unfortunate events when even the innocents suffer. Doubting the fairness of such occurrences, is attempting to negate the Universal perfection and its inherent justice. The unity of the Universe directs man toward "right action." This is the only rule meant to stop the devastation and destruction perpetuated by man. Nature cries along with us, although we are not astute enough to observe its tears. Hell hath no fury like the Universe scorned. According to the Qur'an, when the inevitable Day of Judgment arrives, the Earth will shake and the mountains will crumble.

Because mankind is determined to wreck havoc with the Universe under the name of progress, each individual alone is incapable of halting these actions. As a result, many of us feel powerless. Becoming directly involved in organizations, which fight for the preservation of the Earth, is the first step. Besides educating others, we have to individually honor and revere this abundant Universe, which we are a part of. A materially abundant man who considers himself the winner in his irresponsible fight against the environment, and who must live within an ailing nature, is a badly defeated conqueror.

It was Francis Bacon, a British politician and philosopher, who viewed experimental observation as the true basis of building knowledge. Nature became a laboratory for understanding its secrets. Decartes, a French philosopher and scientist, based on his religious belief of man's supremacy over the animal kingdom, viewed animals as instinctual matter designed to serve man's needs. His dualistic philosophy of mind being separate from matter further harmed the possibility of cooperation between man and his environment. Newton's theories outlined in "Mathematical Principles of Natural Philosophy" published in 1687 constituted the foundation of physics until Einstein developed the Theory of Relativity. The concepts of Newton's mechanics were embraced by the Western world. His laws of dynamics of "inanimate" matter coupled with the more recent discoveries of Maxwell in electricity, enabled man to control the physical world in the name of science to be used for mankind's benefit. Nuclear energy can be man's friend providing him with heat and light, or it can destroy his planet instantaneously. The advanced engineering practices available today can help man to coexist with animated and static matter, or it can slowly destroy his environment.

Contrary to today's irresponsible handling of the ecosystem by various sciences, the ancient spiritual beliefs of people around the world revered nature. The Native Americans believed in the spiritual essence of any being. For the Sioux Indians, the "wakan" represented the spiritual quintessence of the animated and static matter. The Greeks worshipped Gods who were representations of nature: Artemis was their Goddess of Wild Life and Poseidon was the King of the Sea. The

Babylonian myth of creation is the foundation of Genesis, the creation story of the Bible. Although human beings were created in the image of God, it is God who owns the world. The Old Testament contains many verses, which demonstrate God's love for his creatures. Humans have not been empowered to abuse and destroy the Earth. After all, Adam's name comes from the Hebrew word "adamah," which means Earth, and God guided Noah to save the world by telling him to "bring forth with thee every living thing that is with thee, of all flesh, both of foul, and of cattle, and of every creeping thing that creepeth upon the earth" *(Genesis 8:17)*. Although man could eat only plant food in accordance with the first covenant made between God and Adam, after the Flood Noah received a limited permission to eat animal meat. Noah was blessed and told by God that "every moving thing that liveth shall be meat for you; even as the green herb have I given you all things" *(Genesis 9:3)*. Also, God tells Job to "speak to the earth, and it shall teach thee: and the fishes of the sea shall declare unto thee" *(Job 12:8)*.

Throughout history, people instinctually followed many of the above suggestions. Loving the Earth and revering the environment can create man's "Heaven on Earth." Many kings throughout history built Islamic gardens of the spirit, in which wine, milk, and honey were piped through beautiful vegetation meant to simulate the tranquility of Heaven. Eastern mysticism taught man to live harmoniously with his physical environment. The moral attitude of man considering himself one with the Universe is an aim of the Hindus by "becoming one with the Supreme, serene minded, [as] he neither grieves nor desires; alike to all beings" *(Bhagavad Gita)*. It is imperative for modern man to revise his narrow view of separatism from nature. Imposing natural boundaries between species is nothing more than limiting man's capacity to think and act according to the ecological principles of conservation through an inseparable work toward oneness. The eternal reversible change from existence to nonexistence is the core of the Taoism's concept of oneness with the Universe. The belief in Animism is still practiced by Polynesians, who believe that "mana" is a powerful force present in matter. Animism is based on the premise that all things have a soul and should not be destroyed. The Jains, the disciples of Jina, pray to the Hindu gods to be blessed with earthly abundance, and to be guided on the path of moral strength, which prevents them from harming any living creature. The preservation of nature is one of Jains' most important moral obligations. The symbols for some of their gods were animals and birds. The Shinto followers praise the beauty of nature. According to this Japanese belief, Kami are the supernatural protectors of the world through their harmonizing powers.

Lifestyles and architectural practices were created by ancient societies based on their reverence of nature and on the harnessing of Universal energy. Vastu living meant to create a nurturing home for the soul. Supposedly, this practice is six thousand years old. It follows the wisdom of the Hindu Vedas of inviting the divine into man's environment, thus allowing him to live harmoniously within the perfect order of the Universe. According to Vedic philosophy, every form in the Universe is a manifestation of the Supreme Creative Force. The aim of this ancient practice is the creation of spaces, which foster the spiritual growth of man. Vastu honors the elements of life, and treats the home as a space, which must allow a free exchange of life energy between the occupant of the house and his environment. It requires unlimited respect for all living creatures of the Universe. Its unlimited reverence for animated and static matter is proven by the sanctification of each tree, which must be cut with a washed ax before using it in construction. Creatures living in the tree could not be killed. On the contrary, they were invited to leave so no harm would be caused to them. The symbiotic relationship between man and his environment stressed by Vastu practice makes it the ancient root of modern ecology.

Feng Shui has been practiced in China for more than three thousand years. Positioning human habitats in locations that harmonize with the terrain and are aligned with the invisible flow of energy of the Earth is the spiritual thrust of this mystic interpretation of the coexistence between man and his environment. Aligning with the life enhancing energy (Chi) and avoiding the negative energy (Sha), man can be shielded from evil. Modeled according to the Taoist human body, the Chinese believe that the flow of energy through man's living place must be as free as the flow of Chi through the human body's channels. Positioning imaginary animals and birds to protect man's house may be viewed as the unity of life. Modern masters have brought new meanings to this ancient practice. The fortune of the entire human life can be related to the proper positioning of the house. Revering the living Earth and living in accordance with the yin-yang cosmology, Feng Shui represents a sophisticated Chinese geomantic system, which combines astrology with I Ching prophetic power to integrate each individual's life with the natural environment and the Universal order. Ancient Chinese masters understood the importance of living harmoniously with nature as opposed to conquering it. Modern architects and interior decorators use many of the mystical concepts of Feng Shui to enrich contemporary man's life.

Gaya, the Goddess of Mother Earth in Greek mythology, is a deity who was born from the Universal chaos at the beginning of time. She was instrumental in causing the eternal life energy to spiral out of the Earth. Two famous British scientists recently revisited the primitive concept of a living Earth. James Lovelock and Lynn Margulis, at the end of the last century, proposed the idea that the Earth is a living organism, which has its own regulating systems for control of natural balance. They named it the Gaya Hypothesis. The human species, along with the other animated and static components of nature, is a part of this self-adjusting living body. This design is working perfectly to assure the stability and the perpetuation of life. The homeostasis, which maintains the internal stability of all living organisms, seems to be working at the planet's level. It assures the stability of its life through the coexistence of all types of plants and creatures who must adapt to the continuous changes of atmospheric conditions.

The interdependence of the various forms of life on Earth with the environment is considered the backbone of the planet's survival. Although the supporting evidence of their controversial thesis is incomplete, it cannot be directly challenged. It is true that so far the stability of life on the planet has been perfectly regulated by a seemingly divine negative feedback control system with long term viability. However, the automatic "zero-sum game" of gaining life through the increase of some species, which can adapt, at the expense of other species, which are annihilated in the process of evolution proposed by Darwin cannot continue to work. The rapid physical evolution of man and his science has led to permanent damages of other forms of life, thus ruining the self-regulating mechanism of competition. The internal competition between humans, and the distorted view of other species as enemies of man cannot continue. There are no longer available means for the winner to live without the loser. Cooperation between all forms of life in the process of co-evolution is the only road to survival for the already wounded biotic community. Mutual cooperation between life and the environment, in conjunction with man's control of the population explosion is the only remaining relief from the rapid self-destruction of the Earth.

Chemistry, biology, ecology, oceanography, and geology are modern sciences, which enhance their scope by including the concern of preservation of life on the planet. We are more aware now than ever that the environment has a large impact on our health through its direct influence on living cells. Man cannot continue to trespass on animals' homes, thereby chasing them out of their natural habitat. He cannot continue to obliterate plants, pollute waters, and deplete the available oxygen in the atmosphere. As the human species continues to plunder the Universe, disregarding all creatures both human and non-human, diseases resistant to our most powerful treatments will attack us. Unexplained explosions in untreatable diseases including cancer and coronary failure are only some of the effects of the global ecologic collapse. Permanent changes in the weather patterns will continue to wreck havoc on our lives.

As expected, these environmental changes will also be reflected socially in the instabilities of the economic and financial markets. They will become much harder to stabilize as agricultural commodities become scarce, and the population explosion continues to intensify. Food and water shortages, coupled with diseases spread through polluted air and water, will cause endless mass migrations that will signal the end of human civilization. The spiraling environmental decline that is unraveling in front of our eyes will be impossible to be reversed by future generations, as we continue to damage the life boat of humanity. After all, the Apocalypse may come earlier than expected if people do not understand that the end of the world is in sight if changes are not made immediately. If no man can be "found worthy to open and to read the book" *(Revelation 5:4)* with seven seals, then the great Day of Judgment will arrive. We must do everything we can to postpone its arrival. Time is of the essence. While past generations have succeeded to leave unsolved problems for future ones, we must rush to pave the last part of mankind's journey toward perfection for those who will follow us. Preserving our environment is a magnificent way to travel on the last stretch to God.

6

Compassion

o o o o o o o o o o o o o o o o o o o o o o o o o o o o o

"When a man has compassion for others, God has compassion for him."

—*The Talmud*

C ompassion and evil are the two opposing faces of man's free will. Ever since Adam and Eve graduated into the school of life, man has had to choose between these two conflicting behaviors. It has been the optimistic view of some of the greatest thinkers of our time that as we develop technologically, the problem of evil will begin to decline. However, the contrary has proven to be true. From the smallest social unit called the family, to the greatest on the planet called the United Nations, evil activity is either present or ready to show its satanic face at any time. Man has spiraled from the human sacrifice of the weak, which was practiced in the beginning of civilization, to the present modern murdering systems that include automatic machine guns, gas chambers, biological weapons, and nuclear bombs. The human thirst for evil gives a new meaning to the religious concept of sin.

Evil has reared its ugly head many times in the last century. The Holocaust, the Second World War, the genocide in Rwanda, and the "ethnic cleansing" in Kosovo are only a few examples of when man practiced evil on a grand scale. All of us, although not the direct victims of these horrific crimes, have suffered at some time from evil deeds. We need to stop denying evil, look it straight in its ugly face, and understand that evil stems from greed and unhappiness, and not from economic or political reasons. The capacity to have feelings of sympathy and compassion for our fellow human beings makes us human. Free will, the power to reason, and the ability to learn from each other gives us our "humanity." To survive as the dominant species of this planet, every man must work to protect life and eradicate evil. Compassion, forgiveness, and tolerance are the answers. A Yiddish proverb says, "Kindness is better than piety." Always choose kindness!

We are all the same in a number of ways. All living things are identical in that the components of our DNA are the same. Although it may appear that we are physically quite different, we are extremely similar at a cellular level. It is only man's ego, which encourages the illusion of separateness, thus reality continues to be viewed dualistically. It is only through this self-centered attitude that man continues to forge a wedge between him and other earthly creatures. When we are compassionate to our fellow creatures, we begin to understand man's union with all of creation. Although man is the most developed species of the animal kingdom, he still needs to learn from Mother Nature. In nature, species must compete to exist. In human society competition increases productivity, but should never be used to elevate one man above another. Man will never live harmoniously and in peace if he competes for the wrong reasons.

We need to arrest this explosive, competitive, ego-centered viewpoint of "I" versus "you" in favor of a more altruistic attitude toward our planet and all its living creatures. We must realize our oneness with humanity and nature through our intellects, emotions, and souls. Man must see his fellow man as his ally, not as an enemy, or competitor. He must understand that there is enough abundance in this world for everyone if distributed wisely. He must view his fellow man's burdens as his own, and "execute true judgment, and shew mercy and compassions every man to his brother" (Zachariach 7:9).

Having brief glimpses of this wholeness is common to some people. These are moments when they have felt their oneness with the rest of creation, when they have felt that I and everything else are of one essence. This state of consciousness can be experienced during meditation, running, praying, intense emotion or when caught up in nature's exquisite beauty, as when strolling along a beach, watching a bird in flight, or observing a sunset. Although man may realize that at that moment a shift in consciousness did indeed take place, he generally dismisses this experience as an aberration or a waking dream.

If we could move into this permanent shift of consciousness, and internalize our union with the rest of creation, we would no longer function as separate beings with two different perspectives of identity. We could retain our individuality without constantly having to bolster our egos at the expense of others. When one begins to live in this unity consciousness, he is no longer psychologically attached to events in the external world to define who he is. He will no longer feel the need for unhealthy competition, to dominate, and to take more than his fair share, which only results in alienation. He is secure in his sense of self and no longer ego driven. The world continues to turn with its mundane problems, which only affect him superficially. In this state, man is ready to love unconditionally all of Earth's creatures, and not just a select few that he named family and friends.

To love unconditionally is to move toward enlightenment. The Tao Te Ching says: "love the world as your own self, then you can truly care for all things." When we experience this unity, we look at all planetary citizens and earthly creatures with compassion. Our life becomes one of service to others. We become more "other-directed," instead of "I" oriented. As long as society remains steadfast to its extrinsic methods of thinking rather than to the pioneering of inner exploration, very little will change. Man will continue to derive his sense of self from external features, such as physical appearance, careers, friendships, social status, and possessions. He will continue to spend enormous amounts of time trying to maintain his self-image. However, strip away these so called "essentials" and there lies his true essence.

We are here to change this world and find a correct definition of what it is to be good and do good. Being good is not the same as not being bad. Being good implies that we make this world better by doing good. The Universe will always cooperate with us when we are on the right path. Being good is not so hard. Most of us are innately good because goodness is woven into the fabric of our souls. After all, could we take a human life? The answer is a resounding no, unless it is done in self-defense. It is important to define "good" independent of any society. To some people, the taking of innocent lives just because their religious beliefs differ from their own is considered good. Every society produces people who are passionate about a cause. Some will even die for it. Regardless of time or location, one's definition of good should never change. Divine good stands unchanged, regardless of age or society. Compassion is a part of divine good. The definition of good should remain the same whether living in biblical times, during the industrial revolution, or in the new millennium. The same definition of good should stand whether one lives in a democratic society, a totalitarian society, or a socialist society. Good transcends societies and eras and does not change its definition. This is why the Ten Commandments that Moses received from God are so timeless, and will always remain the everlasting code of ethics for Western society. They define the "absolute good." After all, isn't it just as important today as it was in the time of Moses not to kill, and to honor your father and mother? As an intelligent and spiritually developed being, man must search his soul and live his life consistent with the absolute truth. Only then, will he be able to say that "goodness and mercy shall follow me all the days of my life: and I will dwell in the house of the Lord for ever" *(Psalms 23:6).*

Nearly all civilizations have encouraged some form of tithing. Many ancient societies levied a tax upon its wealthier citizens to donate to the poor. Many accomplished and elite people have understood and internalized the neglected principle that we are trustees of the poor. It is a little known fact that Ben Franklin left a great sum of money in trust to

Boston and Philadelphia for philanthropic purposes. He also established several hospitals for the less fortunate.

Agnes Gonxha Bojaxhiu, better known as Mother Theresa, devoted her life to serving the poor and the sick. Born in Macedonia, she trained for missionary work and selected India where she felt most needed. For almost twenty years Mother Theresa taught school but was deeply touched and saddened by the suffering and the poverty she confronted outside the convent walls. She decided to dedicate her life to alleviating the misery in the slums of Calcutta. She started a school for homeless children and was joined by voluntary helpers and soon financial aid began to pour in. In 1950 she started "The Missionaries of Charity" where she not only cared for, but also loved the homeless and the sick. Today, this order has grown to encompass more than one thousand workers. Many of these people have been trained to be doctors, nurses, and social workers.

Mother Theresa was responsible for starting fifty relief organizations operating in India. She selflessly cooperated with others to care for the homeless, the sick, and the dying, regardless of their ethnic background. These organizations have spread to other countries around the world making Mother Theresa a global heroine. She has received worldwide recognition for her compassionate service to others, and is a stellar example of compassion at its highest level. She is a testimonial to the fact that the noblest aspirations of one heart can indeed change the world.

The late Princess Diana, the Princess of Wales, adopted charity work as her royal obligation. She supported numerous organizations devoted to the care of the homeless, underprivileged children, drug abusers, and AIDS victims. She was the Vice President of the British Red Cross and served as a member of the International Red Cross advisory board. Diana is another example of selfless compassion. Although she was royalty, Diana made every effort to ease human suffering. In her short life, she did much to transform suffering throughout the world and to bring love, joy, and peace to all she touched.

Compassionate human beings may lack a broad understanding of the phases of development of the human condition. Although their insight leads them along a kindhearted path, sometimes they may have idealistic expectations of people. They become discouraged and frustrated. Often, compassion is met with suspicion or fear, as people who are reluctant to change or learn greet it with anger and insensibility. Consequently, a compassionate being cannot expect gratitude in return for his gracious behavior. Compassion touches everyone indiscriminately, and without anticipated reward.

Compassion does not always imply an overt action. It is also compassionate and noble to teach someone what he needs to know, thus making that individual self-sufficient instead of encouraging dependency through giving. A compassionate person uses compassionate speech. Words were not intended to be harsh, sarcastic, or mocking. Words are tools, which can be used to help others by encouraging, explaining, or teaching. Articulate language gives man dominance over the animal kingdom. The compassionate man uses it to bring peace, beauty, and harmony to the listener. Words were not meant to be irritating, slanderous, prideful, negative, haughty, or abrasive, as "a gunshot wound may be cured, but a wound made by a tongue never heals" *(Persian Proverb)*. The Universal Law of Cause and Effect teaches that you reap what you sow. Compassionate thoughts, words, and actions delight both the giver and the receiver, charging their being with true happiness. A life-long commitment to compassionate living will always generate an immense spiritual reward.

Man must remember that all material wealth is transient. It will remain here after his physical demise, and another human being will borrow it once again. All earthly possessions were lent to man while here. Eternal ownership does not exist. All that survives on the earthly plane are his reputation and his deeds, both good and bad. On Earth, life will only be happy and fulfilled when balanced both materially and spiritually. Everything in the Universe is cyclical. Giving and receiving are a part of the cycle of life. Giving to others also lessens loneliness and self-centeredness, thus strengthening the bond between human beings. It helps man feel powerful in the face of pain and suffering. After all, when someone's knowledge and creativity advances all of humanity, everyone is able to partake of this achievement to enrich their lives.

Desire in itself is a positive attribute of humanity. It should not be destroyed. Human beings are born to be desirous. The Universe was desirous to create mankind and all the wondrous creatures inhabiting the Earth. As intelligent creatures inhabiting the Universe, we have the propensity to create, to expand, to do more, and have more. The object of desire and how it is used is important. One can desire more money to build a palace or to help feed the poor. Others can desire fame for self-glorification or to promote a worthy cause. Wisdom tells us that no object alone can ever quench the human thirst for more. Choosing the appropriate intention of desire will keep man on the eternal path.

The opposite of generosity is greed. Man's lust for power, wealth, honor, and possessions is like an unquenchable thirst. For some, the more they have, the more they want. As soon as they gratify one desire, they set their sights on yet another. There is no end to this habitual cycle. They spend their whole lives chasing after "more," always wondering why they continue to thirst. This is due to insecurities, weak psyches, and a need to feel superior to their fellow man. The more man craves, the more authentic power he loses. Greedy people are takers, not givers. Greedy people are wealthy materially, but are continually waging war against others. They battle for supremacy, and view their fellow man not as a brother but as a competitor. Greed will always be met with grief and fear. Man must overcome greed with generosity and compassion. Money has no direction by itself. The value of money is determined by its direction.

The most intelligent among us become tangled in money's seductive web when we forget its purpose. It should be used as a tool by which we can make our stay on Earth more comfortable. However, we have come to view money as our source of life, rather than the tool it is. As a result, crimes related to money are treated rather leniently in Western society. Unfortunately, people understand and excuse greed. The media has succeeded in hypnotizing us into believing that we cannot be happy without spending money irrationally. There are many non-material things, which can give us satisfaction. After we afford ourselves a few luxuries, money would be best spent on personal development or worthy social causes.

Money, being a legal institution, has become more highly regarded than ethical behavior. Money brings out the dark side of man when he participates in robbery, fraud, embezzlement, and other money related crimes. Money is neither inherently good nor bad. It is a social institution and not the Universe's gift to man. It should be used for the common good. It is important to understand that a portion of our taxes should be used for social purposes and to lift the circumstances of the infirm or needy. Lifting the standard of living of the lower class makes good economic sense and is our social responsibility. When we elevate the standard of living of less fortunate nations, we lower the threat of violence and retaliation due to jealousy and hostility.

We of Western society have all tasted the milk and honey of money as well as its evils. One should never forget that money could be lost, appropriated, devaluated, and deflated. Money will always remain unstable and therefore should not be regarded as a measure of a man's worth or the meaning of life. Furthermore, as our standard of living continues to rise at an astonishing rate, it seems one never has enough to "keep up." What used to be considered the luxuries of life are now deemed by many to be its necessities. It is in this case that the poor are better off than the rich. The poor man supremely appreciates even a small amount of good fortune. To take the stance, however, that all people should have exactly the same things and the same amount of money is too simplistic. Historically, in societies where equal parcels of farmland were distributed amongst its members, few families ever starved. However, such economic systems did not allow its members to rise above subsistence levels.

Money should be used not only to enhance the life of an individual, but of a group. Instead of causing division and anxiety, money can allow us to show compassion and care even for those whom we have never met. Money is one of the ways by which we can effect benevolent change and enrich our lives as well as the lives of others. When one does not give generously, it shows a lack of trust in the Universal order, which continues to provide the necessities by which to live a comfortable life. Trust does not imply that we can be indolent and all of our needs will be provided. Trust implies that we have been supplied with the physical, mental, and emotional tools needed to succeed in life.

We must remember that the Universe meant for us to be the executors of its wealth and it is not up to us how it should be distributed. Man is different from the animal in that he desires to own material goods. Animals may use goods when needed, but do not understand the human concept of ownership and what it implies. We were meant to be responsible for our fellow man. It only makes sense that the Universe entrusted mankind to distribute the fruits of the Earth and the fruits of his labor righteously. We need to allocate our money for positive ends. There are many people who are unable to care for themselves. They are sick, crippled, mentally deficient, or elderly. When one is blessed with good health, it is his social responsibility to help those who have been less fortunate.

There are those who do not work, but earn their money through investing. Investment is necessary in our economy to allow companies to succeed and grow. However, these people need to appreciate that it is the work of other people, which enables them to increase their fortunes. It is their duty to contribute to society in any way, which would promote the well being of its members.

Greed has also led to many destroying the environment and natural resources, all in the name of money. The environment is not ours to waste, but to be used responsibly while we are here and in so doing protect it for future generations. There have been times when even farmers have destroyed part of their crop in order to keep the prices high. This manipulation of the agricultural market is a blatant example of greed. The ability to buy or acquire an object does not give us the right to destroy or waste it. Raw materials are not inexhaustible. Perhaps it is time to ration raw materials in order to preserve them.

In primitive societies, all goods were distributed evenly so that everyone received their fair share. Therefore, the standard of living of your neighbors would be similar to your own. This prevented resentment and hostility. Today we have moved beyond the level of economic self-sufficiency. We are now able to acquire goods and services, which are not necessities of life. We no longer have allegiance to our fellow man, as did our ancestors. We must rely on our own skills and capabilities. It has become a "dog eat dog" world. There are those who lead lavish lives while others are destitute or living at the subsistence level. Although developed nations have implemented social services to help the aged, sick, or needy, the gap between the rich and poor continues to widen. This schism will cause civil unrest and gives the less privileged a reason to hate the more fortunate.

We all come to Earth with different physical and mental capabilities. Also, luck and opportunities are not equally distributed. It is not an appropriate attitude to believe that one has been blessed with wealth due only to his ingeniousness or industriousness. One must be grateful to those who guided and supported him in developing the opportunities created by the Universe. There is a divine plan for each of us. There are many who seem to deserve more materially and have much less. However, we must be grateful for what we do have, which is far more than in previous generations. It seems that gratefulness and contentedness are appropriate responses to the Universe for our blessings. Only in this way can one curb his jealousy of others who seem to be more fortunate. Furthering economic advancement should never be the primary purpose of life.

Spending money is not evil. Money is an arranged device through which man can interact with others. The Universe is the arranger of the world and has provided abundantly for us all. Silver and gold were mentioned in the Old Testament as a means of trade. "End when thy herds and thy flocks multiply, and thy silver and thy gold is multiplied, and all that thou hast is multiplied" *(Deuteronomy 8:13)*. The elite of biblical society believed gold to be extremely precious. "And the gold of that land is good…" and is placed close to paradise *(Genesis 2:12)*. Because gold is of "divine nature," the possession of gold is not criticized in the Old Testament. In the New Testament, Jesus saw nothing negative about receiving money to "buy those things that we have need of against the feast; or, give something to the poor" *(John 13:29)*.

Religions and organized beliefs used improperly have managed to cause division amongst humanity. Instead of each of us viewing our fellow man as a brother, we view him as a Hindu, Buddhist, Christian, or Jew. These labels separate us as we are convinced that our beliefs are the only correct beliefs. The Universe is primarily interested in making us realize our humanness and in so doing we can transform the world. When we are of service, especially to those who are very different than we are, we bridge the chasm that separates many of us. It is our social and moral responsibility to help others around the world. It is not our right to determine who deserves our help as anyone in need equally deserves. Through our money and the giving of our time, we can effect change at home and in foreign lands around the globe. Compassion is a magnificent way to travel on the last stretch to God.

7

Forgiveness

o o o o o o o o o o o o o o o o o o o o o o o o o o o o o o o
"Forgive others, and then you will receive forgiveness."

—*Muslih-ud-Din Saadi*

F orgiveness has been the neglected virtue in human moral development. Although the Bible is brimming with stories regarding the
success of divine forgiveness and person-to-person forgiveness, it
wasn't until the last decade that forgiveness began to receive recognition as a significant factor in physical, spiritual, and psychological healing. In the past, it seemed forgiveness was regarded as a religious
obligation, with most of the benefit received by the offender, rather
than the forgiver. However, it is now recognized by social scientists and
theologians alike that forgiveness can be a promising mode of healing
and often very much needed for self-preservation. Forgiveness is a healing process, involving several steps, not a one-time event.

Forgiveness means that you completely pardon someone's grievous
act. Forgiving is a personal action which releases the one offended from
the bitterness and resentment incurred from the offense. In this way
the forgiver often benefits more than the offender who sometimes may
be unaware of the offense committed, or of the harm incurred by the
offense. Forgiveness can be experienced on a personal level as well as
being a valuable tool by which to arrest the violence amongst people in
different nations.

Forgiveness and pardoning in the legal sense are not the same. Pardoning in our justice system is a legal way of releasing an offender from the consequences of his actions. Therefore, the individual receiving the pardon has not necessarily been forgiven, but will not receive a penalty for his crimes. Forgiveness can be more difficult when the offense committed is violent or a crime of major proportions. In these cases one may forgive, but justice needs to be served and the offender given a penalty.

Ideally, forgiving implies reconciliation, but this is not necessary for forgiveness to take place. If one or both parties are not interested in reconciling, this does not in any way diminish the profound release often experienced from anxiety, anger, and grief that the injured party may experience. Forgiving only paves the way for restoring harmony in the relationship. Even when there is a lack of reconciliation the forgiver can still benefit, but it is ideal when both parties agree to reconcile. When one forgives, this does not mean that the hurtful behavior can be wiped from his consciousness, or that he in any way justifies or dismisses the hurtful behavior as insignificant. However, the injured party must be assured that the offender has taken the offense quite seriously and will not continue to repeat the same behavior. Sometimes, forgiveness can occur spontaneously and does not have to involve both parties. One can forgive someone without the other's knowledge.

Forgiveness often takes time as the injured party goes through several stages. This involves confronting his anger and identifying the behavior that was hurtful. It also involves a decision to forgive and to not seek revenge or retribution. Furthermore, one must be convinced of the personal benefit derived from forgiving. The forgiver, in his heart, should extend good will and release any negativity toward the other and strive to find purpose in the experience. Perhaps this could mean that one begins to realize that we are held accountable for our words and actions. It is also imperative that the wounded party not let this past indiscretion dictate the future.

Sometimes due to the nature of the crime or indiscretion and the relationship of the individuals involved, total forgiveness is not possible. One should then strive for a fractional degree of forgiveness. In these cases, when trust has been shattered between two close individuals, it may be very difficult to achieve complete forgiveness. Although there is a reduction in the negative feelings and the relationship is restored, the bond of trust is not completely repaired. One can only hope that in time, a new bond can be forged and total forgiveness can become a real possibility.

Mistakes and poor choices may be one of the downsides of living in a free society. Because we are ego dominated and each of us sees the world through our own personal lens, it is highly probable that we will either intentionally or unintentionally cause damage or hurt feelings to those we love. It would be much easier if we could delegate the responsibility for our actions to our government, clergyman, therapists, or scientists. We would, however, due to our inability to handle moral uncertainty, be robbing ourselves of our free will. Good and evil are part of the Universe's plan to get man to exercise his freedom responsibly, and in so doing increase his moral fiber. It is easier to forgive when we are able to reinterpret events and to see the situation from the other person's point of view, without putting a personal spin on it.

It should be remembered that only humans have the complicated task of navigating their way through innumerable choices, decisions that other earthly creatures don't have to think about. After all, animals live significantly less complicated lives. Food, safety, and procreation are their only concerns. They live mainly by instinct. They mate and many times they leave their partner. Their offspring come to Earth already knowing many of the things that humans need to learn. Human life is a much more complicated endeavor. It teems with decision-making. Choices that challenge us both socially and emotionally, such as choosing a life partner, selecting a career, raising children, and preparing for old age make our lives more complex. We are also capable of feeling a sophisticated array of emotions which animals are not privy to. Animals do not need to grapple with decisions that require a great deal of knowledge, nor do they have to negotiate with a highly developed conscience.

It is a human paradox that often we can show mercy and compassion to others, but refuse to extend the same courtesy to ourselves. We need to judge ourselves less critically for being human. We must learn to forgive ourselves. We will be unable to forge genuine intimate relationships with others as long as we dislike ourselves. We need to accept that we are works in progress, and unable to be perfect. We are not innately evil. We must release our pent up remorse, guilt, and regret. Forgiving oneself is a spiritual healing, and can be very liberating. When we refuse to forgive ourselves, the negative impact of carrying around such an enormous burdensome weight can be quite self-destructive. Unresolved guilt and hatred toward oneself results in a loss of self-worth and can be replaced with self-loathing. One can easily become depressed and hostile toward others, and sometimes resort to self-destructive behavior.

On the contrary, self-forgiveness can be a gift to oneself and a spiritual cleansing. As long as a lesson has been learned, we may be able to view the indiscretion in a positive manner and experience tremendous moral growth. Releasing the demons within frees up energy to be used more compassionately in the future. Therefore self-forgiveness is a necessary tool through which to strive for balance and growth. We cannot change past events. However, we can choose to use them as a catalyst for inner growth. When one finds the experience meaningful and uses it to alter future behavior, perhaps then the experience can be interpreted as worthwhile. We always need to separate our identity from the mistake we made and to make a conscious choice to change. Remember, a mistake is an action we took, not who we are.

From the moment we leave our mother's womb, we are confronted with our separateness from the rest of mankind. We are no longer "one" with another; we are now facing the world totally alone. In our desperate search to identify with someone or some group, we often misunderstand what our goal in searching for love or acceptance needs to be. Instead of looking for a way that we can give of ourselves, we concentrate on making ourselves more desirable. Men seek power and wealth while women strive to make themselves more attractive.

When we fall in romantic love, the ecstasy we experience only stresses how lonely we were before. However, this oneness which we feel with another human being after some time, begins to pall. Without work, the unity experienced and the exhilaration disappear and are replaced with boredom and disappointment. Love fails when we don't assume an active role. Love takes work. If one wants to be a good carpenter, teacher, doctor, or scientist one must study the theory of his craft and then practice. However, we refuse to study love, what it is, and how it can be sustained. We are too busy trying to make ourselves loveable and looking for someone to love, and who will love us back. We spend all our energy on earning money and collecting power and prestige. Love is supposed to be effortless.

Man is a part of nature, yet at the same time he is separate. Unlike the animal that lives "instinctively," he was both blessed and cursed with the ability to reason, self-awareness, and the knowledge of his mortality. He is aware that his life and the lives of others he loves will come to an end. These unfortunate facts make him feel helpless and alone. Therefore, man continually strives to rid himself of his isolation by reaching out to others. This is universal, regardless of who we are and where we live on the planet. This is why we join clubs and try to conform in our appearance, feelings, and thoughts. Although we live in a democratic society, and we think we march to our own drummer, generally we conform to make ourselves feel less alone. We feel the need to reduce our anxiety about our separateness, and to relieve ourselves from the boring routine and prefabrication of our lives. Our passion for fusion with another person is the fundamental force driving man.

One needs to understand that love is an activity primarily composed of giving rather than receiving. When we give freely, without any sense of sacrifice or self-denial, we are able to experience exquisite joy and personal power. We can give materially or spiritually. Giving in love is giving in the higher realm. When we love someone, we share our intimacies, knowledge, passions, wit, understanding, aspirations, joys, and failures. In so doing, we enrich the life of another person and abate our loneliness. When giving to another, we enrich the life of someone else, and this joy is reflected back to us because "the value of a man, should be seen in what he gives, and not in what he is able to receive" *(Albert Einstein)*.

However, giving is not enough. Love implies care, responsibility, and respect. This is the arena in which most people fail. We can say we love our pet, but if we don't bother to feed it, this is not love. It is when we don't actively work at a relationship using care, responsibility, and respect as our guides, that we find ourselves in need of forgiveness. Love is a verb, implying action. It grows with time when together two people experience the joys and disappointments in each other's lives. Showering loving words upon someone is only a small part of love. This is secondary to the recognition and respect of each other's uniqueness and individuality. We must remember that when we exploit another human being, or rob them of their dignity, integrity, and self-esteem, we are not demonstrating care, responsibility, and respect. Because we are not perfect beings, when we fail in one of these areas in our relationships, we need to recognize our mistake, change our behavior, and ask to be forgiven.

Forgiveness can be a valuable tool. When hatred and animosity surround a situation, perhaps acceptance, compassion, and forgiveness would be a better approach than a return of retaliation and vengeance. Today studies are being funded to investigate the potential of forgiveness as a political tool in healing social wrongs. Pope John Paul II advocated the principle of forgiveness when he issued a plea for Christians and Muslims to forgive each other. Websites and international studies have been set up to study the reconciliation and forgiveness process. Together with financial assistance packages offered to war torn countries to rebuild their economy, and improve their standard of living, it now appears crucial that when an entire population has suffered, the value of a healing process involving forgiveness and compassion cannot be overstated. Forgiveness is a magnificent way to travel on the last stretch to God.

8

Happiness

"Most folks are about as happy as they make up their minds to be."

—*Abraham Lincoln*

Supreme happiness is the state of bliss achieved by total fusion with the Universe. There cannot be happiness in solitude, selfishness, egocentrism, and hunger for power and control of others. Supreme happiness can be harbored only through a relentless effort to conform to the absolute truth. Because of the continuous dynamics of daily life, it is easy to lose sight of the fact that the happy moments of earthly life are only milestones on a successful journey to perfection. Therefore, being focused toward its elusive end makes it even more distant. When one misses the road to the intended destination, useful time is wasted. Precious happiness is lost when the Universal map is not followed. Every unhappy moment is a waste of human life. Trying to approach supreme happiness is a journey through many lives of adaptation and learning. Those who do not believe in life after death can never approach supreme happiness. On the earthly plane, happiness is the continuous striving to lead a "purposeful" life, along with the forging of intimate relationships in the absence of pain and sorrow. It is an ongoing journey of correct decision-making, seeking pleasure and contentment, and experiencing satisfaction when a state of mind regarded as desirable is attained.

It is urgent to realize that finding happiness in a pure state is not possible. The temporary manipulation of one's reality through any physical means will not lead to happiness. It will just become a deceiving addiction followed by self-destruction. Since ancient times, alchemists have been searching tirelessly for the transmutation of base metals into noble metals without success. Just as platinum and gold are usually extracted as a by-product of common natural alloys, the precious state of happiness can also be attained only as a by-product of good deeds and a moral outlook on life.

Much progress has been made by science to prolong the earthly life, though physical immortality will never be achieved. This has been a human quest since the beginning of time. Taoists believed that gold had the ability to cure diseases. Arab alchemists continued the efforts of the Chinese to discover the elixir of life. A positive attitude toward life, satisfying work, inner self-esteem, supportive family and friends, well spent leisure time, unwavering faith in positive outcomes, and a relentless effort to internalize the need for patience in all endeavors are only a few of the stepping stones on the endless road toward happiness in this world.

In man's efforts to obtain happiness, it is not always possible to avoid pain. Without pain, one would be unable to appreciate the emotion of happiness, as "who has never tasted what is bitter does not know what is sweet"(German proverb). Those who believe that their physical stay on Earth is their only life race to rack up pleasurable experiences at a frenzied pace. They have yet to distinguish between happiness and pleasure. After all, man cannot obtain something for which he does not have a correct definition. What is the difference between pleasure and happiness? Pleasure can be created through recreational activities. Of course this time is necessary to "recreate" and refresh the body and the mind. As modern people chase excessive pleasure after pleasure without consideration for humanity and nature, they continue to wonder why happiness eludes them. Once the irrational party of delusion is over, and reality sets in, the unhappiness of living with the consequences begins. Although pleasure can add to our happiness, it alone will not fulfill us and make us happy. As life's pendulum swings to the other side, one can suddenly find that excessive pleasure can often lead to unhappiness. Drinking feels good but leads to poor health and severed relationships. Alcoholics and drug addicts are not happy people, although they have a great deal of pleasure.

Happiness is commonly being confused with an unrealistic state of continuous joy, amusement, and carefree living. This incorrect definition remains the most serious delusion facing humanity today. As a result of the irresponsible efforts of modern society to obscure the real meaning of happiness through the encouragement of egocentric behavior and endless material satisfaction, man looks for instantaneous emotions of elation. His fruitless search has extremely destructive effects on the physical and psychological expression of life. Divorce, the use of drugs, and illicit sex are only symptoms of humans' lack of happiness. These are psychosocial diseases, which result from the enormous behavioral dimension of the desire of people to experience pleasure.

According to Freudian analysis, the state of felicity derived by the unenlightened, when they become active participants in life's daily contrasts and confrontations, as opposed to the enjoyment offered by the static state of each moment is one of the causes of unhappiness. We must learn to live in the present. This view supports Buddhist philosophy. It is necessary that one must sometimes suffer in order to appreciate happiness. Often, this is the price paid for lack of knowledge or wisdom. The continuous attempt to escape suffering, encountered on the descending side of the never-ending wave of life, brings us to the understanding of the Aristotelian view of real happiness: the full ownership and control of wisdom, insight, and virtue.

It is easy to forget that a "merry heart maketh a cheerful countenance: but by sorrow of the heart the spirit is broken" *(Proverbs 15:13)*. The megalomaniac and the ignorant are always caught in a web of rage as they try to achieve happiness by searching for fame and recognition, and by climbing the miserable social ladder. At the expense of the other members of a group, or of an entire society, narcissists cover their ingrained inferiority complex with pride for their actions and self-delight with their emptiness. Hitler, Stalin, and other mentally deranged historical figures derived pleasure from their deplorable acts. One needs only to look at today's society, beginning at the work place and finishing on the international stage, to locate different versions of people with poor character, who have absolutely no consideration for anyone or anything as they rush to capture the sugar coated pill of unhappiness. Persecution based on race, belief, gender, or skin color generated through the misuse of power, by misrepresented religious doctrines or by totalitarian regimes of government, brought people to the only country in the world based on the "unalienable rights" of individuals. All people are entitled to "Life, Liberty, and the Pursuit of Happiness" as stated in the Declaration of Independence, drafted by the committee led by Thomas Jefferson. It is clearly stated that we are endowed with the right to pursue happiness. However, we are not guaranteed it, and because we are not created equal, as an idealist may believe, it is man's right to seek happiness while not harming anybody or anything else. Happiness is the product of endeavor. It is not God given, only God permitted.

Individuals with unrealistic expectations are often ready to destroy everything for a temporary boost of their ego. Being convinced that they deserve the world, they suffer from a superiority complex. Declaration of unjust wars, terrorist activities against civilian targets, destruction of companies, and the irrational dismissal of capable employees are reported on a regular basis in today's news. These despicable acts stem from the sheer sadistic pleasure of miserable people, who dishonestly obtained a position of power. How many times do we have to misunderstand our position in the Universe to finally conclude that the illusion of happiness, which results from harming others, is bringing us closer to the Messianic end? How many acts of terror, insensitivity to the needs of our fellow man, and inconsideration for the balance of nature are needed for humanity to see the light? The outcome of such acts is the irresponsible destruction of what was perfect in the first place in the name of improvement through restructure. The laws of economics will always correct the asymmetries created by a free, and thus reflexive society. After all, these laws are modeled after the balancing principles of the Universe. Is not supply and demand in economics the human face of action and reaction in physics? Humanity is a part of nature, and it is meant to function in concert with nature. As the disturbance of the food chain, driven by the unnecessary hoarding of food by the never satisfied man, can bring famine to, and extinction of some animal species, the violent acts of man against man, driven by the accelerated run for illusory happiness, will bring the destruction of humanity.

As life unravels on its long and winding road, the truly happy moments will result from correct decision-making and seizing unexpected opportunities. Happiness is not a project, which can be designed. It will develop as serious effort is focused on fulfilling a desire designated as good. Therefore, it is important to choose achievable goals, which are commensurate with one's aptitude. Any other choice would be an endless frustrating journey. In trying to tailor his destiny, one must be aware of his abilities and follow Napoleon's view of achievement: "All that one is able to do is to be a man," while doing "all that one would like to do is to be a god." Although imagination is much richer than reality, it is sometimes needed to change one's self-image in order to discover the road to happiness. When the inability to achieve an ideal dream is substituted with the capability to adjust to reality, the journey toward happiness can begin.

Happiness is a byproduct of a purposeful life. Aristotle suggested that "making progress toward the attainment of our goals" constitutes a large part of the feeling of happiness. His observation is based on the fundamental purpose of human life, which implies serving others in their progression toward truth and unity. Most humans have multiple purposes, and these can change with their age and stage in life. Life ebbs and flows like a wave. It is loaded with many moments of satisfaction. These are the times of contentment. When life's purpose is lost, human life becomes meaningless. However, happiness is not an emotion that can be sustained indefinitely, and any attempt to overextend it will fail. We all have small irritations during the day when we are less than happy. These are moods, which are fleeting and should not be confused with our normal state of mind. It is also difficult to be in a happy frame of mind after a tragedy. Although one may grieve for a long period, a happy outlook will eventually resurface.

Looking at life's successes initiates a broader view of human existence. It is important to capture the entire picture of one's life, not just a missing piece. It is human nature to concentrate on what we do not have and not on what we have achieved. We can look at a beautiful puzzle with only a small piece missing, yet that one piece is what we will fixate on, completely ignoring the beauty of the rest of the puzzle. That piece may belong to someone else's puzzle. There are always other pieces, fitted to substitute for the missing one.

Happiness can be produced through the adoption of a positive attitude toward the world and unequivocal trust in the perfection of the Universe. Happy people have an "abundance addiction." They look for the sublime in the mundane, and appreciate the simple pleasures available to everyone each day. A happy person looks for abundance in the minutiae of daily life. When at life's crossroads, such an attitude expands the power to reason characteristic to human beings, thus focusing all their available wisdom on making appropriate choices. "Happy is the man that findeth wisdom, and the man that getteth understanding" *(Proverbs 3:13)*. Nobody can be certain of any outcome—one can only deal in probabilities. The human intellect will always work to solve an unwanted outcome, and help man navigate successfully through life.

Many people understand that if they have to choose between happiness and money, then happiness is the correct choice. However, more and more people still spend their lifetime chasing material wealth, but will not spend one day studying the meaning of happiness so that they can approach it in their lives. There are many opinions as to what gives us happiness. The unaware individual looks to things outside of himself. Although fancy homes, cars, large bank accounts, or expensive vacations offer temporary pleasure, they stop very short of providing lasting happiness. When viewed at a superficial level, these things give physical comfort. However, none of these externals offer lasting happiness to the perpetually confused seeker of soulful wholeness. The selfish desire to have more at the expense of others in countless attempts to satisfy an ever-growing ego is just a delusion, which always reveals itself later as a form of guaranteed misery. No material thing can ever be a substitute for true communion with other human beings and with nature as a whole. Although this premise is as old as humanity, few people are ready to follow the right path to happiness, which is so well captured by Buddha: "Happy is he who has overcome his ego, happy is he who attain peace; happy is he who has found the Truth" *(Angutara-Nikaya)*. Complete renunciation of all material things is not what happiness is all about. Physical moderation combined with knowledge can guide man towards supreme happiness. According to the Talmud, "the Shechinah (image of God) does not alight in the midst of idleness, sadness,…but in the midst of joy."

Some individuals have most or all of their material desires fulfilled, and still don't feel complete. They rationalize that there must be something more to acquire or purchase and then they'll be satisfied. This cycle, if it continues to habituate, leaves them feeling as though they are caught in an endless loop of chasing their own tails. It is often the individuals with an abundance of material wealth who are spending a great deal of time on the psychiatrist's couch, as happiness continues to elude them. They refuse to follow the old saying that "you cannot always have happiness, but you can always give happiness."

Success and happiness are not synonyms, although in some instances they can be. For the utterly perplexed, the image of success represents financial and material prosperity at any cost without regard for others and for nature. Financial success is only a small ingredient of happiness, although you can be happy without being financially successful. The enlightened individual understands that happiness includes some material comfort. However, without a life of purpose and intimate relationships, without an attitude of gratitude, without giving to the less fortunate, "successful" people remain unhappy. These are people who are stuck on a low level of philosophical development, who think that the title of the James Bond movie, "Live and Let Die" constitutes the right way to live. Now, more than ever, with the exponential increase in population around the globe, and life's basic commodities being exhausted at a maximum rate, the "Golden Rule" can offer us a way to prolong our existence on Earth. According to all religions, the magic of happiness comes from sharing. In Jainism, man should treat *all* worldly creatures, as he wants to be treated himself. This is the most general form of the concept of altruism presented in a religious belief *(Sutrkritanaga)*. Hinduism *(Mahabharata),* and Buddhism *(Samyutta Nikaya)* reduce the Golden Rule only to human relationships. All monotheistic religions adopted this law of high morality in various forms. The most commonly quoted are the words of Jesus: "And as ye would that man should do to you, do ye also to them likewise" *(Luke 6:31).*

Some people, after years of work or struggle, see through the illusion of material happiness, and they understand that you can't love something that can't love you back! They have achieved the fundamental understanding that beyond a comfortable style of living, more material wealth won't make them happy. They realize that intimate contact with another soul is a part of the answer. As we enter the new millennium, married life is becoming more complicated. According to Martin Luther, "there is no more lovely, friendly or charming relationship, communion or company, than a good marriage." However, married people need strategies in order to preserve their union. As both men and women work longer hours, it is difficult to find enough time to give to their spouses and children, let alone find time to pursue their own personal interests. Still, married people must find time to nurture their relationship. Otherwise, at a later age, when their children are gone and their careers are over, they will be facing each other as strangers instead of bonded souls. Marriage can be compared to attending school – you either learn or you fail. It cannot be otherwise, as everything is always changing. If a married couple neglects that bond, their marriage contract will probably expire before its time. The marriages that survive are those in which both partners grow together intellectually and morally. Being an inner feeling, happiness becomes apparent externally in various recognizable forms. Physical attraction, total trust, and an ever-strengthening friendship throughout time are only some manifestations of happiness. Partners must nurture some common interests during their marriage in which they both participate, aside from raising their children and pursuing their careers.

Although children can provide joyous experiences to their parents, and spouses can travel together through times of joy and sorrow, no person or thing outside of oneself can give happiness. Joy is contagious, while happiness is private. Within the dynamics of being, bodies are continuously changing, thoughts and moods are changing, while the human intellect is either growing or declining. How can anyone who is in a constant state of flux, living in a Universe that is always changing, give someone else happiness? The answer is simple: it can't be done. The wife or mother who lives vicariously through her husband and children inevitably winds up disappointed. She needs to develop herself and her interests. Her purpose for living must first be a dedication to herself. Her husband and children can then be an additional source of satisfaction to her. An individual should never be burdened with the impossible task of making someone else happy. It is the purpose of man's earthly life to learn and enrich his soul. Either through inheritance from the time of slavery, or through the misuse of language, we still label people with the word "my." The word "my" implies possession. No one can truly own anyone; we belong only to ourselves. Happiness cannot be achieved through possession. On the contrary, it can only be achieved through freedom.

Humans, like all of nature, are capable of functioning without marriage. Marriage and family are conventions that humans created for convenience, sociability, and protection. Animals don't marry. Due to their biological instinct to reproduce, they mate and then separate. Because of their sociable nature, humans organized the institution of marriage as an extraordinary vehicle of convenience, in which passion substituted for instinct and reason substituted for irresponsibility. Marriage can bring tremendous satisfaction and pleasure, which in many cases produces happiness. Being of human nature, and not of divine nature, marriage can fail as any other written contract can. The dissatisfaction experienced when ending a bad marriage many times can become the springboard for a new period in which happiness can flourish. The human species was created fully capable of living independently. A person without marriage and children is privy to the same completeness as the married one. He or she is blessed with unique gifts and is able to lead a purposeful life. The happiness achieved through married life is generally the result of an ideal match or hard work and compromise between two people. On rare occasions, it can be a successful exception produced by an adventurous endeavor.

Happiness is also a result of positive attitudes and correct reasoning. Correct reasoning leads to appropriate action. How do we define appropriate action? It is acting based upon reason, not on emotion. Emotionally driven decisions usually result in regretful outcomes. Choices made during states of anger or depression invariably lead to destructive consequences, even though they may seem correct at the time. Appropriate action is sometimes painful, but without a doubt is right. Punishment, when appropriate and reasonable, develops character and molds personality.

Positive thoughts are guaranteed guides to a happy life. The Universe will help anyone by responding "in kind" with what the individual's thoughts are. Thus, if one thinks negatively, there is a remote possibility that he will have positive experiences. Most likely, by absorbing more negative energy, a chain of negative experiences will follow. After all, the Universe, being non-judgmental, will serve back to the seeker what is offered to it. Negative thought patterns and undesirable characteristics of greed, hate, envy, deceit, prejudice, and hypocrisy will only serve to reinforce these types of experiences in the earthly life, and interfere with the pursuit of happiness for which everyone aspires.

Since all of mankind is connected, it would be incorrect for any philosophy on happiness to advocate that man should seek isolation. To live by oneself and be concerned only with oneself is a wasted life. Man proves his need for social support by seeking out companionship. Human beings need intimacies, thus by "baring our souls" we are forming a bond with someone. Membership in groups where the individuals promote a certain cause, or share a common interest can easily abate loneliness. A life without intimate relationships, either with family or friends, goes against human "nature." We are all members of the Universe, and we cohabitate. The trees grow near other trees, the grass grows together, and animals travel in herds for protection. Loneliness is a self-created, unnecessary affliction. As creatures inhabiting the Earth, we must "join hands" for the preservation of the human species and for creating happiness around us. As a unified group, humanity has survived, improved, and transferred knowledge from one generation to the next. Because "many hands make light work," we can now afford to relax, learn, and enjoy life's gifts to man. Could anyone, as one individual, have built and devised all that mankind has created on this Earth?

Human creativity is what defines us as individuals. It is the special "stamp" that distinguishes human beings from other animal species. Without the uniqueness of the human inventive spark, man would still be living as the primitive man did during the Stone Age. It is the pooling and the sharing of our creative differences that has allowed, and will continue to allow society to grow in the arts and sciences. It is impossible for man not to create. Man can do this through his intellect or intuition. Highly educated people can create in the sciences and humanities. These are creations of our intellect. Other creations come from the subconscious mind filtered through the intellect. It is the intuitive sub-conscious mind that inspires many novelists, artists, and musicians. When man creates, he becomes one with the experience. He loses himself in his inspiration. Man can create physically as when building a house, assembling a car, or growing a garden or he can create intellectually in a laboratory or in front of a computer. Man is happiest when he is creating. It is everyone's responsibility as inhabitants of this planet to preserve and enrich it. Many people are fortunate to hold social positions where they are purposeful, and they are able to use their creative abilities. Their work becomes their passion. This is how our Universe meant us to live – passionately.

One of the enemies of happiness is boredom. Boredom is a trait of the psyche. People who are bored often get lost in the "doingness" of life, and forget that they are human "beings." We need all our lives, at every age, to be purposeful. People, who feel that in some large or small way they are also contributing to the greater good, feel better about their work and look forward to a happier future than those who labor only for the money. People who work only for their paycheck soon realize that "all that glitters is not necessarily gold." Man feels happiest when he knows he has an impact on the world and when he is doing something that makes a difference in someone else's life. He feels happiest when he joins nature in its most awesome creations. No amount of money or physical pleasure can ever equal that satisfaction.

One should never forget that the brain does not age as the physical body does. Living a creative and constructive life must be the main consideration of today's modern man. Purposeful lives are happy lives. Either in the work force or during retirement, man must create and be convinced that he can leave an individual legacy of his temporary earthly existence to the generations that follow. With the significant increase in man's life span, the retirement period has to change its meaning. No human being can strive for happiness in a state of continuous relaxation. The rapid change in the modern life style, which was produced by recent developments in science, engineering, and medicine, requires a redesigning of the last period of our earthly presence. Recreation must become what retirement used to be. "Re-creation" means creating again. It does not imply repeating our youth. It assigns value to the wisdom acquired throughout life. Retirement without a plan, which interweaves recreation with continuous learning and contribution, is doomed to have an unhappy ending. For some, it may even become a psychological "Hell on Earth," as humans are meant to live with purpose.

History proves that people derive a great deal of satisfaction and happiness out of work or hobbies. Age and creativity are not exclusive. Grandma Moses used her mental faculties throughout her late years. She was seventy-six years of age when she began to paint. She lived to be one hundred, and her portraits are still displayed in major museums. Michaelangelo created many of his great works beyond the age of eighty, and Commodore Vanderbilt added one hundred million dollars to his financial empire between the ages of seventy and eighty-three. Oliver Wendell Holmes wrote "Over the Teacup" at approximately eighty years of age, and John Wesley continued to deliver moving sermons beyond the age of eighty-six. These people realized the wisdom in the bible when "They shall still bring forth fruit in old age" *(Psalm 92:14)*.

It is every man's right to seek happiness, and it is his obligation to be a part of the oneness with the Universe. In this trying time of unrest around the world, the ability to live a life of purpose, thus preserving our planet, elevating the individual soul, and the souls of others is now more important than ever. Happiness is a magnificent way to travel on the last stretch to God.

Epilogue

"If you go to heaven without being naturally qualified for it, you will not enjoy it there."

—*George Bernard Shaw*

A t our present level of scientific development, it is not possible to perfectly time Creation, nor is it possible to know what precluded the first moment of Universal existence. The "Grand Unified Theory" is being developed by physicists to create an integrated explanation of how everything began and where we are going. While this extensive scientific effort is under way, we have to deal with our preservation within the Universe. Being inhabitants of one of the planets of the Milky Way, we are only temporary materializations of Universal Energy. In this form of existence, as tenants of the earthly natural complex, it is our duty to preserve the life on our planet.

The future of our physical life seems bleak, as the human race continues to follow the road to destruction. While the sun can still give us heat and light for at least six billion years, we need to prolong our time on Earth in order to revolutionize the present system of combustion of spacecrafts, such that they will be able to transport us to other planets and stars. Unfortunately, such a grandiose project cannot be attempted when famine, disease, environmental destruction, lack of faith, and localized wars poison our stay on the planet, and as ignorance and conviction to terror limit our time on Earth. The number of depleted human souls is increasing in an explosive reaction of birth, life, and death in subhuman conditions. Crime, terrorist activity, and the irrational destruction of natural resources are only a few symptoms of our present social decay. If the prophecies of Nostradamus can be trusted, then the next global war will claim the lives of more than half of the Christian, Jewish, and Muslim population.

Time is running short. Can we make the ultimate effort to preserve what we inherited from our parents, to create happiness, and prolong the period before the unavoidable Apocalypse? While every religion has described the Armageddon in various terms, they all provide the same solution: the complete destruction of the world followed by a reconstruction led by a Messiah. It seems that famine, drought, and the appearance of new incurable diseases, coupled with wars driven by distorted religious beliefs are fulfilling the prophecy of Shambhala. Chaos, lust for material wealth, and useless power over our fellow man are signs of a very treacherous end of human existence. The Jews are waiting for the "Day of the Lord" when a new world will be inaugurated. The Christians are expecting the return of Christ after all the sins of humanity are eradicated. According to the Sunni Muslims, the prophet Muntazzar will unite all people on Earth at the end of time. Every Hindu anticipates Krishna's final incarnation as a new avatar, which would bring order to a world of chaos. Maitrya Buddhais will come to awaken the consciousness of every Buddhist and Shinto believer. These are scriptural images, which can help us to maximize the potential of the spirit we acquired from the Universal Energy Spectrum. They represent unequivocally the shared enlightenment of all mankind. As future initiators of a new world order, they can be viewed as the divine remediation for mankind's sins at the end of the world. However, the Messiah is in all of us. Thus, it is our responsibility to make the final stretch of humanity's journey toward Universal perfection a glorious rally to the elusive finish line.

About the Author

Marian Barasch is an internationally recognized expert in vibration analysis. Holding Master of Science degrees in Mechanical and Nuclear Engineering from the University of Houston and Renssellaer Polytechnic Institute, he is currently teaching Physics at Hudson Valley Community College and Vibration Analysis at the State University of New York. He is a successfully published technical author and a member of The Philosophical Society of England.

During his technical and scientific career, Barasch was awarded one U.S. Patent and has been listed in the Millennium edition of the "International WHO'S WHO of Entrepreneurs." His formal scientific training and his acquired philosophical knowledge allow him to view the mystery of life from various vantage points. He lives with his wife and their two children in Albany, New York.

To learn more about this book and author, visit
www.marianbarasch.com

0-595-25777-1